DIGITAL
DISRUPTION

DIGITAL DISRUPTION:

UNLEASHING THE NEXT WAVE OF INNOVATION

JAMES McQUIVEY

FORRESTER RESEARCH

amazon publishing

Published by Amazon Publishing
P.O. Box 400818
Las Vegas, NV 89140

ISBN-13: 9781477800126
ISBN-10: 1477800123
LCCN: 2012921030

INTRODUCTION

I t's not just you. Things really are changing faster than ever before.

At Forrester, we've been tracking technology trends for more than twenty years. The difference is that now, they're not just technology trends. They're consumer trends, and potent ones at that. Today, customers use technology as a lever to exert more and more power over the companies. Are you ready for this?

Companies used to get dominance through scale. In the first half of the twentieth century, that scale came from manufacturing, and companies like GM ruled. Later in the century, dominance came from supply chains (think Walmart) or information mastery (think Amazon). But in the twenty-first century, none of these sources of scale matter. Only customers do. This is truly the age of the customer.

In this age, old strategies, such as locking in customers, are passé because those customers can read reviews on a mobile device and switch allegiances in an instant. The only source of competitive advantage now is a focus on knowledge of and engagement with customers.

A new breed of competitors has arrived: digital disruptors. These companies and individuals embrace digital tools and platforms to get closer to customers and engage them more deeply. These competitors can come from anywhere and, unopposed, they will steal your customers and disrupt your business.

As James McQuivey shows in this groundbreaking book, preparing for a world like this requires a new mindset and new set of behaviors—one that creates a perpetual customer connection even as it embraces disruption. This mindset may have originated with digital disruptors, but as you'll read, even big old companies like Disney have embraced it.

Prepare yourself. What James has to say is not comfortable to read, but it may well be the best tool you have to prepare yourself for the coming disruption.

—*Josh Bernoff, SVP Idea Development,*
Forrester Research, Cambridge, Massachusetts

CONTENTS

PART 1

What Is Digital Disruption?

1

Digital Disruption: What It Is and What It Means for You

This book is about the fundamental change in our lives that will be caused by digital disruption. In these pages we will prove that digital disruption exists, demonstrate how it can be used by anyone in any industry, and implore you to make yourself as ready—as disruptive—as you possibly can be. Why? Because digital disruptors are turning our world—and your industry—upside down.

What will digital disruptors do? They'll help you lose weight, then they'll help you decide how to do your hair on a Friday night. They'll make your child's violin lesson really soar. They'll deliver you a morning report of the time you spent in REM sleep. They'll help your business glean one hundred times as many insights from its customer database at one one-hundredth the cost. They'll help you treat major illnesses, or better yet, they'll watch you 24/7 and identify your risk for illness before you even fall prey to it. They'll help you figure out which Thai restaurant is worth trying out at the same time that they warn you that your teenager took the car to a neighboring town when she should have been in school.

Value comes from seeing what customers need and delivering it. Digital disruptors will do all of this at lower cost, with faster development times, and with greater impact on the customer experience than anything that came before. To prove this, I'm going to go all the way down to the lowest unit of analysis. I'm going to introduce you to the youngest possible face of digital disruption.

———

Thomas Suarez is a typical twelve-year-old working his way through the sixth grade in the South Bay area of Los Angeles.[1] He describes himself this way: "I've always had a fascination with computers and technology." *Always* for him goes all the way back to the fourth grade, when Thomas decided that he wanted to program something.

His first app, Earth Fortune, went live in 2010. It has been rated 127 times and earned a respectable three-star rating in the iTunes App Store. It's a fortune-teller that's kind of cute, a bit like the origami "cootie catcher" we used to play with when we were in grade school, that told arbitrary fortunes to those willing to believe them. But the story here is not the app, it is Thomas himself and the many Thomases yet to come. Young Thomas gave a talk at the Manhattan Beach TEDx conference in October 2011, during which he explained, "My favorite and most successful app is Bustin Jieber, which is a Justin Bieber Whac-A-Mole!" This app was posted just before the holidays in 2010, and while it hasn't earned as many reviews as Earth Fortune, it certainly garnered laughs from the TEDx audience.[2]

Bustin Jieber won't change the world. The top review, last time I checked, gave it one star and called it "crap," adding that, "When u take money from me for crap, I'm upset no matter how old u r. Put down the programming books and read up on user experience and usability and then sell something for a dollar." The second review gave it five stars and said, "I just donated $99 cents [*sic*] for your future games ;-)." While they disagree, both reviewers are taking seriously the fact that Thomas is a twelve-year-old app developer.

If you just play his apps, you might be tempted to discount Thomas. You might conclude that the two million views his TEDx video has scored on YouTube or the write-up about Thomas in the *Huffington Post* are just hype.[3] But the real story is best illustrated with a third review— another five-star rating—which read, "I had $1 left in my iTunes account and decided to spend it on this, just because I'm just like you. I'm 13 and trying to learn iOS/Cocoa development, and this is really encouraging. Thank you."

Why did Thomas's talk garner two million video views? Listen to what he says:

"A lot of kids these days like to play games. But now they want to make them. And it's difficult, because not many kids know where to go to find out how to make a program. I mean, for soccer, you could go to a soccer team, for violin, you could get lessons for a violin. But what if you want to make an app? Where do you go to find out how to make an app?"

Thomas explains how the iPhone SDK (the software development kit that Apple makes available for app developers) "opened up a whole new world of possibilities for me. And after playing with the software development kit a little bit, I made a couple apps, I made some test apps." One of them was Earth Fortune. When he was ready to put his new app up on the app store, he had one last hurdle to clear. "I persuaded my parents to pay the ninety-nine-dollar fee to be able to put my apps on the app store. They agreed, and now I have apps on the app store."

And this is the point. The distance between an idea and the digital realization of that idea is now so short—so cheap and so quick—that a bright twelve-year-old can do it.

Let's compare this to how things were in 1981, when I was twelve. At that time, I took my life savings out of the bank to buy an Atari 400, the most sophisticated computer I could find for my paper route money. I had a BASIC programming language cartridge that I practically burned out coding for hours, learning how to create text scripts, poke values into system RAM, and eventually make a maze game—the pinnacle of my BASIC programming experience. Total cost: five hundred hard-earned dollars. Not a lot of money, even after you index for inflation or the pain of delivering newspapers in the snow. In sharp contrast with Thomas, my programming career gained me nothing but self-satisfaction.

If I wanted fame—or anything but obscurity—I had to type up my BASIC code on a typewriter and mail it in to *BYTE* magazine hoping that they would publish my submission so other people could replicate the code on their Ataris, if they were so inclined. There was no SDK, no uploading, no App Store, and certainly no TEDx conference or YouTube.

Even years later, when I bought my first Windows 3.0-based computer and started programming in C, there was no SDK. I had to make my own buttons and hard-code my own user interface. When the SDK finally came out more than a year later, it cost hundreds of dollars over and above the C libraries and compiler I had already sunk my money into. And if I wanted to distribute my code and make money from it? Ha! You get the picture.

That's why so few of us who grew up in that era pursued computing as more than a hobby. We didn't have access to the tools, neither the hardware nor the software. And don't point to Bill Gates, Steve Jobs, or the other whiz kids who eventually generated the software and hardware innovations that made modern computing possible. Without exception, all of those industry giants had early (and sometimes unauthorized) access to powerful hardware and systems that the rest of us not located in Seattle or Silicon Valley lacked.

My point is not that I could have been Bill Gates. My point is that I and thousands like me never really had the chance because we never had the tools.

Thomas and his thirteen-year-old reviewer on the App Store have access to the tools. And they have the right mindset, one that compels them to use these tools in *disruptive* ways. They are the next step in the evolution toward a digitally disruptive economy—a world in which everyone has the tools they need to bring their ideas to the market, test them, refine them, and eventually disrupt something.

What tools does Thomas need to pursue his digitally disruptive goals?

A computer? Check.

An internet connection? Check.

A programming language and SDK? Check.

A friction-free digital platform for distributing and making money from his innovations? Check.

The number of homes in the United States that have a computer with internet access is now better than 77 percent.[4] The SDK is free. And the

App Store entry fee is $99. Thomas and a good portion of his generation have access to better tools than Bill Gates (or I) had. Just as millions of kids already grow up playing soccer or learning a musical instrument—comparisons Thomas invoked, very appropriately—millions of kids like Thomas will routinely learn how to engage in digital disruption.

And at almost no cost. The right mindset combined with the right tools, continuously adapting and disrupting. Multiply Thomas by millions and you get a sense of why digital disruption is so terrifying.

—————

This is not a book about twelve-year-old entrepreneurs. It's a book about how digital tools allow digital disruptors to come at you from all directions—and from all ages, backgrounds, and nationalities. Your competitors probably won't come from within your industry—they could come from any industry, or from one that doesn't exist yet. Equipped with a better mindset and better tools, thousands of these disruptors are ready to do better whatever it is that your company does. This isn't just competitive innovation, it's a fundamentally new type and scale and speed of competitive innovation. And it will totally disrupt your business, even if that business has nothing to do with digital. Because the mindset may be digital and the tools will definitely be digital, but that mindset and those tools can be used to disrupt any industry faster than old disruption could.

Ralph Waldo Emerson supposedly said, "Build a better mousetrap and the world will beat a path to your door." That's a true statement. People who say this usually apply it to innovation generally or to invention specifically. But the core truth of the phrase is about neither. Invention is a fine thing, but thousands of things have been invented—indeed, the US Patent and Trademark Office has granted more than five million utility patents, those granted for inventions rather than just processes or ideas, since 1963.[5] But inventions alone don't create huge value. Not unless they disrupt something.

Recast in terms of disruptive innovation, the truism might become, "Disrupt the mouse eradication business and the world will beat a path to your door." Less catchy, for sure, but this version reveals two facts about historical disruption that have always been true: 1) Those disruptions do best that are aimed at a core benefit the end user understands; and 2) For most of history, disruptions occurred in a physical world of factories and well-trod distribution networks.

When it comes to core benefits, remember that building a better mousetrap is not the point. Trapping mice also isn't the goal of the end user. Mouse eradication is the goal. Go a level deeper and it's about protecting one's environment from harmful influences, generally. At yet another level, it's about survival. This is important because disruption means finding a better way to meet a *fundamental need* that the customer has, not just replacing an existing process or outcome with something similar but slightly better. That hasn't changed and won't change. In fact, it will only become more important.

What has changed about invention is this: disruption was previously done *to and through* physical things, things like the assembly line, the commercial jetliner, the heart transplant, flat-panel LCD screens, and so on.

These physical disruptions are just as important as the digital disruptions this book focuses on. But because traditional disruption depended on changing how physical resources were manipulated or combined, the disruptions, though powerful, were *rare*. They cost a fortune to develop and distribute, a fortune that kids like Thomas Suarez simply would never have.

To put this in context, let's look at the seminal work of Harvard Business School's Clayton Christensen, the father of the concept of disruptive innovation. Beginning with his 1997 book *The Innovator's Dilemma*, Christensen brought the topic of disruptive innovation into the minds and mouths of business practitioners around the world.[6]

Clay describes how a disruptive innovation is an advance that creates new market value, in the process disrupting and replacing an existing market. With illustrations from the disk-drive industry and the hydraulic excavator market—both very physical markets—he shows how disruption starts with cheaper or more convenient solutions that gradually move upmarket, eventually destroying stable industries.

Clay shows that the traditional disruptive innovations he studies typically take years or even decades to disrupt markets. As his case studies show, physical disruption requires the painstaking manipulation and alignment of physical resources. The resources themselves are often expensive, as is the factory that makes the new product. They can only become profitable by achieving scale, and scale requires massive initial investment to succeed at disruptive prices, and this holds whether you're making a mousetrap, a CD player, or an electric car.

This takes time. And it takes money—lots of it.

Digital disruption will change that. But not just in software or apps. In fact, the power of digital disruption is that it can disrupt any aspect of any product or service, including processes deep within companies focused on physical things, processes that govern partnerships, data collection, pricing, and the management of labor or capital resources. In fact, digital disruption's power multiplies precisely because it can apply to industries that are not even digital. In this way, digital disruption happens *to and through* digital things, which then accelerate the disruption of physical things. Take Guy Cramer, who uses digital tools to get better military camouflage designs to governments around the world, faster and way cheaper than other suppliers. Then there's Travis Bogard, head of product strategy at Jawbone, a company that pivoted rapidly from bluetooth headsets to mobile speakers, challenging accepted notions of what consumers want from an audio product and then creating a best-selling speaker in the category it redefined. Dave Dickinson, CEO of Zeo Inc., found a way to rethink expensive ($3,000) studies in sleep labs by offering a hundred-dollar product you can use to analyze your sleep every night, right at your bedside. These disruptors know that digital disruption is far more potent than old disruption, regardless of the industry.

These cases, and more like them, will show that digital disruption beats old disruption hands down, no matter the industry. It does this in a straightforward way. Under old disruption, only a very small number of innovative companies can amass the tremendous amount of capital necessary to develop and bring a small number of possible ideas to market. Capital is the first constraint. You can raise capital through bank loans or IPOs or private investment, but as long as you have to spend money to make money, the market can only fund so many innovations.

The second constraint is information. Because only a few ideas will make it to capitalization, people keep ideas secret, floating only those ideas that have immediately obvious economic merit. And the only innovators who get funded are those who have access to holders of capital and are willing to jump through whatever hoops investors deem necessary to prove their ideas have merit.

But what if it didn't take money to make money?

What's terrifying about the digitally disrupted future is that this rhetorical question is already being concretely answered. The mindset of the digital disruptor accelerates every possible process by exploiting digital toolsets that are free for tinkering. Economists talk about trends that reduce barriers to entry. The force of digital disruption doesn't just reduce these barriers, *it obliterates them*. This allows the disruptor to take new ideas of any size and potential impact and rapidly pursue target customers at almost no cost and in the space of a few days, rather than years.

That's the power of digital disruption, and it will happen to every industry on the planet, whether that company makes digital products or not. That's why the rise of millions of digital disruptors like Thomas Suarez, whether they go it alone or choose to disrupt on behalf of massively physical firms like Verizon and Unilever, matters so much. These disruptors will do what they do in whatever industry they find themselves planted, ultimately generating significantly more innovation power into the marketplace.

How much more innovation power? I'll make it as simple as possible.[7]

Imagine that with all the free tools and platforms available to Thomas Suarez and millions of others like him, we get ten times as many people bringing innovative ideas to market—a highly conservative estimate. Then assume that the average cost to develop and test those ideas falls to one-tenth as much per idea as in the past (also conservative). The result would be one hundred times the innovation power (see Figure 1-1).

Figure 1-1: Digital Disruption Creates One Hundred Times the Innovation Power

That means you and your business are facing *at least* one hundred times the competitive threat. That's two orders of magnitude more innovation power than before. Digital disruption accelerates competing ideas even as it facilitates the entry of a previously impossible number and magnitude of ideas. The cumulative effect is devastating to any company operating under the rules of the prior century.

Consider an analogy: what China did to the manufacturing business. China is now poised to overtake the United States as the largest economy in the world. It has achieved this position principally by becoming a low-cost manufacturing center for goods the rest of the world desires. But China's success is not just a function of cheap manufacturing, the way Japan, and later Korea, rose to prominence in the twentieth century. China's success depends on a very fortuitous (for China, anyway) set of circumstances.

First, with its population of over 1.3 billion relatively impoverished people, China has a very motivated base of workers who are willing to work very hard for very low wages relative to other parts of the world. Add to that the fact that these workers can expend their efforts to produce and distribute goods using technologies, distribution partners, supply chains, and physical infrastructure, such as international shipping companies and container ships, that China didn't have to pay for because the rest of the world had already seen fit to create them.

Meanwhile, the American manufacturing companies that China was competing with had high labor costs and rigid structures that required them to keep working pretty much the way they always had. China leveraged its advantages and its competitors' inability to change. It came in and decimated its manufacturing rivals.

Let's condense this. The formula is: People willing to work for nearly nothing, plus a completely developed, relatively friction-free infrastructure for value delivery, equals competitive disruption. People + infrastructure = disruption. That two-step formula is sufficient to explain the rise of China and the subsequent destruction of much of American manufacturing.

What's happening now in digital is completely analogous *and much faster.* Worldwide, there are even *more* people like Thomas Suarez, willing to work for practically nothing. And like the Chinese, they can take advantage of a digital infrastructure—already built by some of the world's most powerful companies—to launch their work into the world and see what happens.

If you thought the impact of the rise of China was tremendous, the rise of digital disruptors—toiling away for free in any country, speaking any language, coding for whatever platform they deem worthy of their time—will be far more comprehensive across more industries at a more rapid pace, just like China's impact on US manufacturing, but across every industry.

The friction-free infrastructure that they will leverage includes the Apple App Store, which has already generated 650,000 apps and $5 billion in payments to thousands of developers.[8] This friction-free infrastructure is spreading like a virus to many other domains. Facebook's developer platform is a similarly powerful global outlet for idea generation, generating more than 9 million Facebook apps.[9] If your innovative idea is not one that can be developed in software alone, you have the emerging Kickstarter fundraising platform to pitch and refine your concept, as more than twenty-eight thousand people have done, receiving $274 million in pledges.[10] If your powerful idea is not about a product as much as it is about how to market and communicate an existing idea, you can register as an individual to advertise your site, your app, or your eBook through Google

AdSense or Facebook Ads. Want to set up your own shop to sell your own or others' products? You can join 1.3 million sellers on eBay or you can sign up as an Amazon-enabled merchant. These friction-free elements of the digital world are scaling up in every domain, drawing wannabe digital disruptors rapidly into the fold.

If people + infrastructure = disruption, then digital innovators + digital infrastructure = digital disruption. *Massive* digital disruption, at a scale and a pace most are simply not prepared for. Sometimes people make themselves feel better about their lack of preparation by pointing to specific failures along the way, such as the falling stock price of Facebook after its IPO or the inability of Groupon to figure out its business model. But behind them are thousands of others willing to take their places. It's all part of the process. Just as in China, where the occasional failure of a single factory or centrally planned community amounts to a minor glitch in the overall outcome. This will be true of digital disruptors as well.

Digital disruptors fail frequently. When I propose that there will be one hundred times the innovation power resulting from the rise of digital disruption, I realize that the majority of those additional ideas will come to naught. Some will fail spectacularly. But if ten times as many people can participate in bringing ten times as many ideas each to market, only one or two percent of those ideas need to succeed in order to completely disrupt your business. And what if their success rates are five times that high? That would be half the success rate of typical venture capital investments. But it would be five times the *volume* of successful idea generation that you currently experience.

That's innovation power defined. Because if you pick any single example of an idea generated through digital disruption, you may or may not be impressed. Thomas Suarez's Bustin Jieber app, for example, may not move society forward. But it *does* move Thomas Suarez forward—on to his next app, which will certainly be better than the one before. At the rate he's going, he may have twelve more apps under his belt by the time he graduates from high school, or he may have just one more app that is twelve times better. Again, multiply him by millions and you have some sense of what is coming and why it will generate innovation power that should motivate you, hopefully into joining the ranks of the digital disruptors.

When I talk to executives about the need to do this, they squirm. Because no company will willingly rush into a future in which its assets are made rapidly obsolete and its business processes must continually be revamped to accommodate increasingly uncomfortable digital disruptions. As Clayton Christensen points out, this has always been true of disruption: established companies resist investing in disruption because the economics don't add up for them; in many cases, more financial value will be destroyed than created, even if the industry as a whole and its customers will get more value in aggregate.

My job in meetings with executives—and my job now in this book—is not only to convince you that you do not have a choice, it's to teach you that being digitally disruptive is easier than you think, that it can happen right away, and that by taking small digital steps today, you will arrive at massively disruptive outcomes tomorrow.

I won't leave you to suffer this disruption without a guide. I'm going to show you how to do the three things you must do to succeed in this digitally disrupted world.

1. **Adopt a digital disruptor's mindset.** Digital disruptors don't have to be young, but in many cases they are because their minds were formed in an era when digital possibilities were rapidly erasing analog boundaries. The rest of us came up in business school and industry in an era where the answer to most questions about innovation was *no*. The digital disruptor's mindset is one in which the default answer is *yes*. This isn't the result of sheer optimism. It's an optimism born out of the facts. And it's based on exploiting three elements of today's innovation infrastructure: cheap or free tools, digital platforms, and digital consumers. I'll address these elements in chapters 2 through 5.

2. **Behave like a digital disruptor.** A digital disruptor's mindset may be based on a fundamentally disruptive worldview,

but it's the behaviors that worldview inspires that really matter. Relying on their altered sense of reality, digital disruptors innovate differently, building different products, using a different model for partnership to make it all happen. This starts with a technique we call *innovating the adjacent possible.* Digital disruptors rapidly add adjacent benefits to their product experiences, experimenting with enhancement after enhancement, following their customer's lead to build what is ultimately a completely business-altering—disruptive—outcome. They then flesh out these new possibilities by delivering total product experiences, surrounding their products and services with digital enhancements. I'll explain these core behaviors of digital disruption in chapters 6 and 7.

3. **Disrupt yourself now.** With the right mindset (and commitment) in place to enact the core behaviors of digital disruption, it's time to move your entire organization to disruption. Gone are the days when you can assign this task to the "digital team" or the "mobile guys." Everyone in every level of the organization must accept that they have the responsibility to become digital disruptors within their domain as well as across traditional silos. To do this in any company, you'll need to assess your readiness and determine your best path to digital disruption. I'll show you how to do this in chapters 8 and 9. And when thousands of companies adopt a digital disruptor's mindset, behave like digital disruptors, and complete their own disruption, the stage will be set for yet another accelerating round of disruption. This is the world we will all live in soon enough. I'll show it to you in chapter 10.

I welcome you to the digitally disrupted world. It's a better place to be, as the digital disruptors already inhabiting it can tell you. To write this book, I visited many of them and have come back to report on what it's like to live there.

In this world I see Charles Teague, the CEO of FitNow, Inc. With a total of eight employees, FitNow built and supports the Lose It! app, which has helped over 10 million people track the calories they consume and thus regulate their weight. This little company uses every digital trick in the book to keep costs low while adding consumer benefits one after another, creating one of the Apple App Store's most successful health and wellness apps.

I see Dr. Hugh Rienhoff, CEO of FerroKin, a medical research company that is taking the cost and time out of clinical drug trials in an industry most assume is impossible to disrupt. FerroKin's employees work from their homes, outsourcing most of the lab work and hurdling legal and regulatory barriers with rapid efficiency. Rienhoff and his team of eleven focus like lasers on molecules that big pharma companies can't invest in because they have to pay back their massive cost infrastructures. The possible outcome? Better drugs at lower cost, leading to improved life outcomes.

I see Tim FitzRandolph, lead creator of Disney's smash hit app Where's My Water?, a cute game that in late 2011 took on the international phenomenon of Angry Birds and won, week after week. Embedded in the midst of a media giant, this little team of mobile developers exploited existing skills and resources at Disney to rapidly build one of the most successful game apps on the planet, establishing a new model for Disney to generate and test ideas without cannibalizing any existing products or distribution models.

I see Jeff Hammerbacher, chief scientist at Cloudera, a data storage and analytics provider that uses open source software running on commodity hardware to give orders of magnitude more analytical power to even the largest enterprises. Cloudera analyzes companies' existing, unstructured data and creates opportunities for these companies to take the kinds of smart and responsive steps previously only expected of startups. And Jeff and his colleagues do all of this without a winner-take-all mentality.

I see these and other disruptors that I will profile in this book, along with many thousands more we can't possibly describe in these pages. They are all better, stronger, and faster than you are, but not by virtue of overwhelming investment or business force. Instead, they do what traditional businesses, including yours, had thought could not be done: they take small, focused steps that add up to rapid, massive disruption.

Let's join them.

PART 2

Adopt the Digital Disruptor's Mindset

2

Change Your Mindset to Change Your Business

Digital disruptors think about opportunity differently. Even though technology plays a key role in their actions, their edge does not come from technology; technology is just a means to a different end, an end that most people can't even conceive of because they don't have the disruptor's mindset. Equipped with the right mindset, disruptors naturally see technology and other tools in a different light, one that enables them to see past the problem to the solutions that digital can help them deliver more rapidly than before.

Some industries are nimble and flexible and adaptive—and then there's health care, especially pharmaceuticals. Operating in one of the most analog industries in history, today's drug companies have grown into ossified giants. They invest billions in order to make billions, living forever in the fear that the next drug they invest in will turn out to have harmful side effects or will fail to achieve its hoped-for clinical outcomes.

But as Dr. Hugh Rienhoff knows from personal experience, the industry is still susceptible to digital disruption. He founded FerroKin BioSciences, a drug development company that is disruptively doing everything this industry supposedly can't. The results so far are promising.

By focusing his virtual team on a single molecule—an iron-binding molecule that addresses the problem of iron overload associated with many blood disorders—and pursuing this focus relentlessly, FerroKin recently completed several Phase 1 drug trials in both the United States and Europe and has also completed its first Phase 2 drug trial, targeting a possible launch of the drug as early as 2016. FerroKin's model has proven so effective at rapidly and cost-effectively developing this single molecule that the company was acquired in early 2012 by specialty biopharmaceutical company Shire for an upfront payment of $100 million plus potential milestone-based payments of $225 million more.[1] That's a nice payout for FerroKin's original investors, who originally put in $30 million.

Prior to Hugh's attempt at drug development, this type of rapid development might have required hundreds of millions of dollars to bring to market. More likely the drug would never have been conceived because the specific clinical conditions that this drug treats do not affect enough people to justify spending that much money. It is precisely because of these economic constraints that most of the drugs that pharmaceutical companies develop target large populations afflicted by conditions like heart disease, depression, and, of course, erectile dysfunction. Less "popular" conditions receive little attention.

How can digital disruption solve this problem? Sure, apps and websites can help track patient well-being or facilitate compliance with a doctor's orders to take a particular medication. But they don't treat diseases. If that medication can't be developed in the first place, all the pretty apps in the world won't help.

But Hugh has found a way to make the economics work: a digitally disruptive *shortcut* to more cost-effective drug development.

Hugh ticks off in rapid-fire succession the obstacles that have blocked others. "Every aspect of this industry is unbelievably regulated, as it should be for drugs. But part of the development problem is that there's not one person who can understand the whole process, and as a consequence [that process] naturally lends itself to silos that become very isolated from one another. [People in different silos] typically don't talk, and they also multitask—one regulatory person might be on five projects—so you have a natural fragmentation of responsibilities in decision making."

Hugh looks at each of these structural barriers as a problem that can be solved with a digital intervention.

For example, one of FerroKin's most important solutions to the cost problem is to have no physical office, instead relying on wireless phones and home internet connections to coordinate an intensive round of pre-clinical investigations and regulatory filings. "We wanted to do this from our homes," he says, because putting a premium on being in the same physical location every day and attending endless meetings unnecessarily constrains whom you can hire and what work skills you pay for in an employee. Sensitive medical information can be secured digitally even as it is shared among distributed team members and the outsourced labs and clinics that are performing the work. As a result, digital reduces the barriers to focusing on the job at hand.

Consider the daunting job of managing the sixty separate people across fifteen different countries working for vendors that provide everything from actual laboratory work to paperwork for FDA filings. Much of what these vendors did historically depended on pushing papers back and forth. The bureaucratic tangles that can ensue when these companies have to work together could consume even more time and money. But Hugh streamlined the process with the help of Clinipace, a company that has securely connected to patient databases at hospitals around the country to rapidly identify and recruit potential test subjects. Clinipace also relies on data capture technology at trial sites, collecting the right data more accurately and reporting on it more swiftly. Clinipace shares that data with clients like FerroKin as well as their assembled teams of medical experts for faster—and ultimately more accurate—decision making.

At every step along the way, Hugh relies on digital connections like those provided by Clinipace to accelerate the process even as FerroKin improves it, creating unprecedented opportunities to iterate and refine the ultimate product. Hugh and his team also depended on fundamental digital tools like email to connect with a network of clinicians and expert doctors in the field and ping them on oft-overlooked questions such as what color the pills should be and how many pills should comprise a dose. The digital connections Hugh has built into his virtual organization model ensure that FerroKin can address these questions—and improve the ultimate product—at the same time.

Yet what's interesting about the digital solutions Hugh relies on to disrupt the pharmaceutical industry is how little he even thinks about them. Instead, his disruptor's mindset keeps thinking past the technology to the collateral issues, such as how to staff and motivate an organization this disruptive. "Typically, when you're in a silo, it's underground and all you can see are the walls around you. But if you allow people to take on responsibility, you can see further down. What we deliberately set out to do was to involve all the people in all the facets of the program—clinical, chemistry, regulatory, business development, and animal. They are all aware and can provide input to any aspect of the process from the very beginning. That way everybody is familiar with the whole thing." Digital serves as the bridge to connect all of these people in this fundamentally altered way, and all the documents are posted on a server that any of them can access.

With a digitally disruptive mindset like Hugh's, you actually look past the technology to the problem you're trying to solve. And each barrier you encounter summons another digitally-enhanced response that enables you to change physical outcomes—in this case, treating more people and saving lives. It's this disruptor's mindset that makes the difference.

———

If you work in a company of any size, then it's certain that you work for a company that is in need of significant retooling, situated in an industry that is about to be remade by digital disruption. Yet how many of us have rethought our approach to problem solving from the perspective of digital disruption? If Hugh can disrupt an industry as monolithic and stodgy as pharmaceuticals, you can disrupt your industry, too.

Don't be misled by the "digital" in digital disruption. True, digital disruption depends on the right technologies and the right tools, but it's not primarily about the technologies or the tools. And even though digital disruptors seem smarter, it's not even about how smart they are. Digital disruption is a mindset that ultimately leads to a way of behaving; a mindset that bypasses traditional analog barriers, eliminating the gaps and boundaries that prevent people and companies from giving customers what they want in the moment that they want it. Once digital disruptors adopt this mindset and begin to act accordingly, they just get better—better at seeing ways around, under, over, and through structural and market problems. And they get so jazzed about what they see that, using better and cheaper tools, they get faster, making digital disruption as much about *speed* as about technology.

Hugh Rienhoff sums this up succinctly: "I think that if you can make a decision in a day that would take a week or a month, the whole process is improved."

While the particulars of Hugh's success apply to the world of health care and pharmaceuticals, underneath those concerns I expect that you will find shades of your own experience: your own silos, your own frustrations, and even your own excuses.

Digital disruptors obviously are people with energy and passion for what they're doing. They take digital shortcuts and sometimes break the rules, either implicit or enshrined in corporate policy. But simply being passionate and willing to upset the corporate apple cart does not make one a digital disruptor. Those actions have to be driven by the right mindset.

How do you know if you have that mindset? I'll lead you through a quick (and probably familiar) exercise. Imagine your company has taken you and your team to a picturesque location. There are easel-sized Post-it pads at the front of the room and there may even be a guy like me standing there who has been hired to lead you through a brainstorming exercise. On the whiteboard at the front of the room is written: *How can we make a new product that we can successfully sell?*

Most of us have participated in this type of exercise at least once, and by now the drill is familiar. Through the course of several hours' discussion, you will be asked to define your opportunities in the face of your threats. You'll then prioritize the opportunities, break them down into tasks, assign those tasks to specific teams or individuals, and adjourn.

This is a neutral process: there is nothing inherently brilliant or flawed in it. But from the many sessions of this kind that I have led, I have observed two broad outcomes that tell me a lot about the mindset the company has cultivated. What I typically see is a barrier-based mindset. That barrier-based mindset causes people in the room to read the whiteboard question interpreting the words *make*, *product*, and *sell* in this way:

Make: What is our capacity for making a product we already know how to make?

Product: What is the market for a product we already know how to make?

Sell: How would we position ourselves in that market to win customers we already know?

Naturally, these three questions align with standard business silos in the typical organization: engineering, product management, and marketing. Companies organize this way precisely because these are the problems that have to be solved when creating a new product, whether you are Apple introducing a consumer device like the iPad or a heavy manufacturer like Vestas introducing a new industrial turbine.

Asking and answering this question—*How can we make a new product that we can successfully sell?*—from within these silos is so straightforward that it's hard to question its effectiveness. And if it were 1980 and digital disruption were not yet upon us, we could safely continue asking and answering questions like this for years to come. But it's not 1980 and digital disruption is already here, which means that seeing this question this way is exactly wrong. Let's examine why.

First, it conceals an inside-out approach to product development that is fatal in a digital era. Any company that starts by asking what it can do next will fail to understand what the customer needs to do next. Even companies with large customer research functions typically fail here. I've had a front-row seat to the failure of many companies with very robust research functions, from major retailers to consumer electronics manufacturers to large automakers. In the dwindling years of these enterprises, my interactions with their heads of research have been characterized by a sad and sometimes bitter recognition that even as the organization continues funding customer research, its executives pay less attention to that research. Why? Because they are distracted by internal problems and capacity issues.

The irony of this shift in executive attention away from generating value for customers to salvaging internal processes is that it is the ideal way to ensure that the company won't innovate its way to a solution. Instead, it will self-obsess into oblivion.

The second problem with this approach is that it looks *inside* the organization for the resources necessary to generate the next product experience the customer will require. But this is exactly the reason that existing companies are vulnerable to digital disruption: they are only playing with the tools they currently own rather than expanding their toolset to include everyone else's. This is a profound shift in business. Today, only companies that partner promiscuously can accelerate the delivery of their innovative ideas. Companies that only look inside to find the ideas, tools, and resources they need to generate the next successful product may eventually find some of what they need, but it will take too long and generate too few improvements to sustain the company. Meanwhile, digital disruptors outside the company will connect with each other and with established suppliers and partners on products that rapidly threaten the company's core business.

The third problem is that this traditional approach to innovation fails to understand the product itself. Are you selling a new and improved version of the same product you or your competitors sold before? Or is your best idea something new—something that hasn't been invented yet? And how will you know, if you only look inside to find the answer to that question? Surely your product engineers, focused as they should be on reducing the bill of materials in your current product line, will think their job is to make the same thing, only better.

That's not a bad thing, it's just insufficient, especially in the face of digital disruption. Now let's reconsider the original brainstorming question and see it the way a digital disruptor like Hugh Rienhoff does. Instead of asking "How can we make a new product that we can successfully sell?" the disruptor asks:

How can we give people something they really want?

The subject of the sentence hasn't changed—we're still the ones who have to act on the opportunity, after all. But the ideas embedded in the question have completely changed.

From *Make* to *Give*: Instead of focusing on what we have the capacity to make, we focus on what we have the ability to give our customers, even if it lies outside of our capacity.

From *Product* to *People*: Instead of focusing on the product itself, we turn our attention to the needs of our customers, letting the product decisions flow from that.

From *Sell* to *Want*: Instead of focusing on how we'll sell the product we create, we obsess about aligning the total experience of our product with the customer's desires, giving them what they want, when and where they want it.

This is a benefits-based mindset. In the case of FerroKin, Hugh's customers are not consumers shopping at Best Buy, making a single purchase decision. Instead, his customers comprise a highly complex set of stakeholders that includes employees, lab partners, regulatory experts, lawyers, and medical researchers, each one contributing continuously throughout a years-long process of development and testing. The results so far are promising. By focusing his virtual team on a single molecule for a single set of disorders and pursing this focus relentlessly, FerroKin succeeded sufficiently to get itself acquired and will soon be delivering drugs to help people in need. The success cannot be traced to any single change of behavior. It was a change of mindset that changed the behavior that changed the business.

Just over a year ago, I was asked to join the weekly meeting of a consumer insights and product team at a major manufacturer of computer accessories. I was asked to join because the company was struggling to grow in meaningful ways and the executive team had asked the insights and product team to come up with new product ideas to help spur growth.

We started with a conference call in which the team could tell me about the charge they had been given and what resources they had. They wanted to know what product innovation methods I could offer and how I might help them innovate more quickly. I summarized some of our innovation tools and explained the variety of ways that we work with clients through workshops and other meetings. To help illustrate the point, I applied one of the principles I'll talk about in chapter 6, innovating the adjacent possible, and using that method, I rapidly generated three product ideas that were clearly adjacent both to their customers and their own capabilities. One of the ideas was particularly obvious and, I thought, worth pursuing, so I expounded on it, mostly as an illustration of how the process rapidly yields useful fruit.

That idea—a Bluetooth bathroom scale this company could manufacture and then distribute through partners with health and wellness interests—was so compelling, I found myself listing the names of partners they could work with to get it to market in half the time that they typically develop and deliver new products.

The other end of the phone went silent. "We're not just going to make some random product," the team leader said.

I was stunned, and not because the idea was necessarily the right one for her company. I was stunned because she was clearly in the wrong mindset. While it may well be that her company didn't have the capability to make these scales, saying no to a product benefit your customers will clearly need just because it doesn't fit within your current self-concept is a dangerous basis on which to make product innovation decisions.

The team leader and her team didn't want innovation after all. Instead, they had come to me to find a way to propose a safe product, like yet another wireless keyboard, this one for the internet-connected TVs that other people were making. That was their definition of innovation, because they were coming from the barrier-based mindset for asking product innovation questions:

Make: What is our capacity for making a product we already know how to make?

Product: What is the market for a product we already know how to make?

Sell: How would we position ourselves in that market to win customers we already know?

I don't blame her for having the wrong mindset. It's very possible, even likely, that she was responding out of frustration, the kind of frustration that comes from having watched the executives above her—also afflicted with a barrier-based mindset—reject disruptive ideas in the past without even considering either the ideas or what those ideas could eventually teach them. Unfortunately for this company, while they were rejecting my idea as "some random product," other, more disruptive companies were not similarly inhibited. It was no surprise to me to find that among the most touted products at CES 2012 were the wireless scales offered by Withings and Fitbit—products this company could easily have made and sold successfully.

———

Guy Cramer didn't set out to become the world's largest holder of copyrighted camouflage patterns. He entered the camouflage industry in 2003 as a complete outsider, motivated partly by an interest in paintball. More significantly, he was outraged over the Canadian government's decision to spend millions upgrading the Canadian army's camouflage to

CADPAT, or Canadian Disruptive Pattern, a pixilated camouflage pattern that in Guy's view was a waste of money.

Maybe Guy's mindset was clouded by anger in that moment, but it quickly turned around, allowing his natural tendency to focus on benefits—benefits he could create and deliver using digital tools—rather than barriers. With a few hours of work using an off-the-shelf computer graphics program (one he still refuses to disclose for fear that it will inspire competitors), Guy created his own pattern he called GUYPAT and posted it on the web to make a political point. He didn't know then that his whole life was going to change as a result of his mindset leading him to digitally disruptive actions. But his life *did* change, completely, when someone working closely with King Abdullah II of Jordan spotted the pattern and called Guy.

Years ago, this story would have ended with Guy Cramer as CEO of a multimillion-dollar company with big offices in major cities around the world. He'd have a staff working for him that would fly his lab-tested camouflage patterns in private jets to show to military staffers behind closed doors, billing all of the expense to his clients. He'd be importing nothing but the finest cigars. And the camouflage business would not be cheaper or much better than it had been a decade ago, when he first entered it. Benefits would not have increased, and barriers would not have been torn down.

But that's not Guy's mindset. Instead, he works from a nondescript office in British Columbia. He has a single part-time employee who manages some of the office details, but Guy's pretty much the business. Just as with FerroKin, there's no lab, no expensive testing facility. Instead, in his case, he has a digital archive of more than twelve thousand patterns that he has created and copyrighted, built by combining a variety of known facts about human vision and applying them to different colors to achieve different patterns.

If you have something to hide, there's a very good chance that Guy has already created the pattern that will do the job. With over twelve thousand unique patterns securely stored in his digital files, Guy and his part-time assistant are now in charge of one of the free world's most critical security assets. Today, governments outfitting military troops and hardware call from around the world to ask Guy if, in his files, he has a camouflage pattern that will protect their assets from the eyes of the enemy. Guy has patterns optimized for hiding jets in the desert, troops in the jungle, or tanks in the forest. The "good guys," as he calls them— representatives from the dozen countries that use his patterns, including the United States, Canada, and Jordan—all have him on speed dial. Meanwhile, the "bad guys" expend significant energy trying to uncover any of his latest patterns so they can copy them, or at least be on the lookout for disguised troops protected by them.

If you want to test one of his designs, all he has to do is run some fabric through an off-the-shelf large-format printer to create custom military uniforms in small batches. He then sends these to be tested in the field or directly to a team of, say, Navy SEALs that need a specific type of coverage for a deep mission.

Though what Guy is doing is cool, what's even more powerful is how *simply* he's doing it—and how cheaply. When I spoke to him from his office in British Columbia, he explained it this way:

"I have turned down angel investors—we make more money than we spend. I don't need an IPO, I don't need to bring extra money in." Investors resent his unwillingness to play the traditional grow-the-company game. "You get a negative reaction when people are trying to throw millions at you and you won't take it. People say, if it sounds too good to be true, it probably is." He pauses, then adds, "I deal in that all the time."

Guy succeeds because he has the mindset of a digital disruptor. He figured out, long before the rest of us, that digital efficiency trumps traditional business practices anytime. The King of Jordan has money, but when given the choice, he would rather not spend that money to fly a team of camouflage experts to meet with his military advisers and conduct expensive, time-consuming tests. He needs results faster than that, and at a cheaper price. So thinking customer-first, Guy did all of his initial development for Jordan by uploading top-secret camouflage patterns to hidden subdirectories on a website. He used his off-the-shelf photo editing program to construct a new pattern quickly and cheaply, then emailed a secret link to the Jordanians. They accessed the page and downloaded the file, which Guy then deleted from his servers.

In movies like *Mission: Impossible*, high-tech espionage seems to require a gazillion dollars of tech infrastructure and a team of geek savants who can disarm security protocols with mobile devices that haven't been invented yet. But truth is stranger than fiction. All it takes is straight-up file transfers and email.

And the right mindset.

————

If you can't tell by now, behaving like a digital disruptor will be hard. And I guarantee that you will not be motivated to do it if you have a barrier-based mindset. In fact, you won't be *able* to do it if you have that mindset. Because a digital disruptor's behaviors flow naturally from a digital disruptor's mindset.

Before we dig deeper into those behaviors, we have to start with this: accept that digital disruption is not only *a* possibility for your company's future but the *only* possibility. Once you have embraced that fact, you can then open your mind to the free tools you will depend on, the digital platforms you will exploit, and the digital consumers you must serve.

3

Free the Tools, Free the Disruptors

There is such a thing as a free lunch.

This statement can't be true, it has never been true. Except that when you're a digital disruptor, it *is* true. Not only do digital disruptors inhabit a world where resources and opportunities are available to them for free, but they are so entrenched in the idea of free that they participate in, perpetuate, and accelerate the cycle of free things.

How did they get this way? Many of the digital disruptors profiled in this book are under thirty-five, precisely because that generation was the first to grow up in a consumer economy where free things were not simply promotional tools. Starting with Netscape and Napster, then progressing to HotMail and Gmail, Dropbox, Blogger, Facebook, and Pinterest, this generation internalized the idea of free from the consumer side. This led to the kinds of rapid digital adoption curves that run through the body of digital disruption like arterial supply lines. But even those of us who adopted digital technologies later in life can easily learn to value free digital goods. Everybody loves free.

Digital disruptors apply the love of free things to every business decision they make. Present them with a business or market problem and they not only search out free tools to help them overcome that problem, they then make more free tools available to their customers and even other disruptors. That's the free-tool mindset and it's essential to a digital disruptor.

Combine those two elements—disruptors who use free tools to continually offer more free things and consumers who rapidly adopt and depend on free things—and the result is a perpetual disruption wave.

————

Thanks to Chris Anderson's book, *Free*, there has been ample debate and discussion about the power of business models based on free things.[1] This discussion has introduced words like "freemium" into the everyday business lexicon. But this chapter is not making the point that businesses can and should use free things as a way to attract eager audiences. I'm making a more precise point, one that will go further than mere business models. I'm describing a mindset that is entirely dependent on free things, a mindset that liberates anyone that has it from a myriad of constraints that otherwise hamper innovation. In this mindset there are three kinds of free tools that the digital disruptor easily sees and seizes.

1. Totally free
2. Nearly free
3. Essentially free

1. Totally Free

To understand the power of what is totally free, let's meet Gabrielle Blair, a digital disruptor known to thousands of bloggers and millions of readers around the world as Design Mom.

I got to meet Gabrielle in a remote corner of France, sitting in a quaint farmhouse that dates back to the 1600s. The original flagstone floor created an impression that matched the rough-hewn beams above my head. It's ironic that I would come to such a romantic setting surrounded by countless symbols of bygone eras to meet a digital disruptor. But digital disruptors can succeed from anywhere, including remote farmhouses, because their free tools work anywhere there is an internet connection.

You may find parts of Gabrielle's story familiar. She's a power blogger. If this were 2008, I'd be including Gabrielle in this book to illustrate the power of social media. But it's not her use of social media that I want to emphasize, rather it's her digital disruptor's mindset and embrace of and creation of free tools. It's how she has built several businesses for her-self—her blogging empire and a sold-out conference business—using *free* to generate profits, and in the process, undermining the revenue plans of much larger businesses.

Gabrielle is a designer who worked first full-time and then as a free-lancer in New York City. When baby number five came along in 2006, Gabrielle realized she had reached a turning point. "I know that if I'm not doing something creative, I'm going to get depressed," she explains. Balancing freelancing and motherhood seemed challenging. "So I said, 'What else, what can I do?' My sister Jordan had started a blog, I had been reading hers for a couple of months . . . I saw my sister's blog, it was just a picture with a couple of sentences. I thought, 'I can do this.'" And Designmom.com was born.

After six years of growth, Designmom.com now attracts hundreds of thousands of unique readers a month and can generate as many as five hundred comments per post. Her site is fully supported by advertising. Kraft, boutique jewelry makers, and other design-focused manufacturers and retailers sponsor her posts to reach style-conscious moms.

Blogger makes good—you've heard that story before. But let's look at how Gabrielle's mindset differs from the people who succeed in design at traditional magazines like *Martha Stewart Living* or *Vogue*. At those magazines, after years of kissing up, staying late, and waiting for the people above them to recognize their value and promote them, very few striving to gain influence in the media world attain their goals. But thanks to digital tools—all of them free—Gabrielle, her sister Jordan, and other mommy bloggers achieve media success—financial success—with-out having to climb the arduous corporate ladder. The key to their success is not only using, but giving away, free things.

Early on with Designmom.com, Gabrielle realized that there was one thing she craved even more than revenue—feedback. "I could see I had traffic, but my posts would get three comments." How could she get more? She hit upon a simple concept—give away some earrings. Working with a vendor she had featured before, she arranged to send free earrings to commenters as a way to stimulate reader engagement. She wanted it to be simple. "I wanted to give readers a reason to try commenting, they could say anything at all. You don't have to be clever." By offering free giveaways, she suddenly found she'd "get sixty or a hundred comments instead of three." This helped readers feel part of a community, which created growth.

Within a week, instructions identical to those she had detailed on her website for qualifying for her giveaways started showing up on other blogs. They were copying her straight out, plagiarizing her language as well as appropriating her idea. Her reaction was not outrage, as in a traditional media company, but support. "Blogs copied me right away, most of them sending me an email asking if it was okay. I told them, 'totally.'"

Totally free is a perfect way to summarize Gabrielle's entire experience. She used free blogging tools to create content that her followers could read for free. She gave away jewelry to inspire people to create free content for her site. And she gives other bloggers free advice on how to imitate her—not just that first time but at blogging conferences including Alt, the conference she organizes, where she gives aspiring imitators secrets on how to approach sponsors and what kind of ad rates to shoot for. As she puts it, "There's room for everyone, let's make room for everyone. [At our conferences] we're doing tons of practical classes, how to use your camera, how to write an email to a potential sponsor, how to manage your inbox. These are all real things. I'm constantly telling women to start a blog. At the hairdresser, wherever I meet people. 'It's free, did you know it's free? And if you don't like it, you can turn it off!'"

Gabrielle's free-tools mindset leads to this conclusion: Her free giveaways, free content, and free advice make her a solid living. Solid enough that she could take her family to live in the French countryside, where she blogs about the challenges of traveling all over Europe and buying fresh eggs from the neighbors. She doesn't make millions because as a sole proprietor, she doesn't need to. That's part of the power of digital disruption—taking advantage of totally free tools means that you don't need to become Martha Stewart in order to have a career that looks a lot like, well, Martha Stewart's.

As Gabrielle has learned, and so eagerly shared, making things totally free initiates a self-reinforcing cycle. Companies make tools available for free—like Blogger, Google's blogging platform. The digital disruptors that use those tools, in turn, make their experiences available for free. Consumers do their part by embracing free tools like Pinterest or Instagram. Because consumers respond so vigorously, they inspire new disruptors to think of new ideas, which those disruptors need to develop quickly to stay ahead of the competition. These new developers look for free tools that they can quickly exploit to get their idea made. The demand for new free tools provides incentive for other companies to give them free tools and thus win them as customers. The totally free tool cycle only accelerates, drawing in more participants that create and offer more free tools, all to make a profit more quickly from elsewhere in the business.

This is good because the more tools we free, the more people—and the more companies, including big ones—we free to take advantage of them and to benefit from their use. Apple knows this. You could see it in February of 2012, when Apple announced the iBooks Author tool.[2] This totally free toolset allows anyone willing to agree to Apple's terms of service to create multimedia eBooks for the iPad that can contain text, video, photos, and basic interactivity—all without any programming or coding experience. The tools are free, and if you want to liberate your creative ideas, you can even give your books away for free. Or, you can choose to sell them on the iBookstore, where Apple takes a cut of your sales in exchange for having made you a digital publisher.

Free tools spawn more free tools. So Amazon created the digital self-publishing platform, now called Kindle Direct Publishing, more than three years ago. Signing up for it is free, and using its fairly basic toolset, you can publish your own novel to the community of more than 30 million people that read Kindle books on a variety of devices. Here again, free leads to profit. The list of Kindle self-made millionaires is growing, following in the footsteps of early self-publishing authors like Amanda Hocking, a paranormal-romance author who caused a stir in 2011 when publishers found out she was bringing in six figures every month from a collection of eBooks costing around ninety-nine cents each.[3]

That's the paradox and the power of totally free: It makes some disruptors totally rich.

2. Nearly Free

Pinterest is the classic example of a totally free service, but it would not be possible without the second category of free tools: nearly free. On Pinterest, tens of millions of users "pin" things they find around the internet—pictures of cute kids, humorous internet memes, trendy shoes from a retail website—and their friends can follow their pins, repinning their favorites. It's a social network based around pictures, basically, and it is one of the fastest-growing social networks ever, reaching more than 10 million users in its first two years.

It's the kind of company people love to heckle, however, because despite its tremendous success, Pinterest doesn't have a way to make money. In the dot-com rush of 2000, and the bust that followed it, there were many companies like that. Buy.com sticks out as a memorable example, a company that sold retail products below cost in hopes of building a big customer base.[4] The idea back then was that you shouldn't worry about making money, there would be plenty of time for that later. Then the clock ran out and many of those companies folded, taking millions of investment dollars down with them.

What makes Pinterest any different? Ultimately, Pinterest will have to make money, it will have to find a way to get somebody to pay for something. But one of the company's secrets in the short run—one of the things that allows it to perpetuate the totally-free cycle for now—is that the company knows how to take advantage of totally free and nearly free resources whenever it can. For example, the volunteer labor force of Pinterest users does all the work of curating content from across the web for free, evidently enjoying it. This creates the content that keeps Pinterest interesting and ever-changing to users, without Pinterest having to pay them anything for it. But Pinterest's real leverage—what lengthens its runway to profitability—comes from knowing how to take advantage of a second class of free tools: nearly free tools.

Pinterest has an unprecedented growth problem. Scaling up to millions of users is one thing, but trying at the same time to keep track of every picture, video, or quote they pin is the real challenge. Imagine millions of users, each pinning hundreds or thousands of things. That amounts to billions of web objects that Pinterest has to track, identify with the right users, associate comments with, and analyze to figure out where the actual revenue opportunities might lie.

This free service sure seems like it should cost a lot to maintain. And if this was the year 2000, the company would already be bankrupt. But since we live in an age that offers as many nearly free tools as totally free tools, Pinterest can turn to Amazon Web Services (AWS) to not only provide the server capacity needed to rapidly scale up the business, but to also manage much of the data analysis the company needs.

Steven Armstrong, senior analyst relations manager at AWS, explained to me how Pinterest ran all of its server needs through AWS, allowing it to keep up with its unprecedented growth on the backs of only nine staff members, two of whom worked in the IT department.[5] Usually, to save those kinds of labor costs while maintaining reliable uptime, you'd have to spend more on services, not less. But because AWS was founded with a digitally disruptive mindset, the exact opposite has occurred.

Steven explained that since its launch in March of 2006, AWS has actually lowered its prices nineteen times. And during that time, the company has continued to improve the service while continuing to drop prices for customers. In 2011 alone, AWS added eighty-eight major features to its offerings, never once raising prices.

The spirit of nearly free applies everywhere else in a digitally disrupted landscape. Incorporating this thinking into their unique mindset, digital disruptors expect prices to fall and have a knack for finding tools, resources, and services that will dramatically reduce their own costs at startup and beyond.

Naturally, Pinterest needs to find a revenue stream. If other similar companies like Twitter and Facebook are any guide, a broad and active user base can generate hundreds of millions of dollars from very light advertising, especially advertising that fits in a simple and nonintrusive way into the stream of updates. But the point is, Pinterest can move carefully to generate a revenue model. Why? Because it has generated millions of users and rapid growth with nearly free services and tools.

3. Essentially Free

The last category isn't really fair, but it's not about digital tools. I include it because in case after case, when I'm talking to companies that operate with a digitally disruptive mindset, they inadvertently betray a dependence on this third category of free tools. These are crucial to their success, even if they don't realize just how crucial. Simply put, essentially free tools are resources that are free to you, because you already had them lying around, sometimes literally.

That's what Tetra Pak, a company that supplies packaging for beverages sold around the world, found out. Take this Gatorade bottle I'm about to pop open. It's actually the result of six years of intensive research and innovation. This new bottle holds one of Gatorade's G Series line of beverages, this one a post-workout recovery concoction that I'm sure an actual athlete would benefit from. But I don't care about the beverage today. What I'm interested in finding out is how the bottle opens, how it feels when I hold it to my lips, and whether I suck, pour, or pull. I'll explain.

Tetra Pak makes a variety of beverage containers from juice boxes to half-gallon jugs for milk. Their packaging is effective at protecting a wide variety of beverages during packaging, storage, and delivery. These packages can be found in 170 countries around the globe, delivering more than 75 billion liters of fluid in 2011 alone.

In 2004, Tetra Pak came to the design and innovation consultancy Continuum Innovation with a problem. Their packages were great for storing and pouring, but except for using a straw, they had not been specifically designed for drinking. The trend to a more on-the-go lifestyle meant that more people wanted to drink from the package, which meant that Tetra Pak needed to find a solution to compete with plastic bottles and cans. These challenges caused Harry West, at that time a design strategist and now Continuum's CEO, to go all the way back to the basic question at hand—what makes people satisfied with their experience of drinking from a bottle? What makes for a great drinking experience?

Harry's team analyzed all the research that had ever been done about how people drink. What they found was astonishing. There was no research. No matter where they searched, Continuum's team could not find any studies that describe how people drink in general or what makes for a satisfying drinking experience in particular.

The ideal study, had it existed, would classify the ways that people drink. It would involve watching people drink from containers and categorizing the different ways people do it. Continuum could have designed and launched a study just like that. But it would have taken time and money and there was no guarantee that it would yield the knowledge Continuum needed to advise Tetra Pak.

In the spirit of essentially free tools, Harry reasoned that even if a full-blown study wasn't feasible, there had to be a cheaper way to achieve at least similar results. This was the kind of thinking Harry's team at Continuum had learned from its rapid prototyping lab facilities and equipment: They had learned that if something didn't already exist, they probably had the tools to make it, either out of foam or lightweight wood or by printing it on a 3D printer. But in this case, the thing they needed was knowledge, not a prototype. That's when Harry decided, in the absence of a formal study, to simply begin watching people drink, starting with the essentially free resources he had on hand: a bottle of water, an old webcam, and Harry's own gullet.

They started by cutting out the bottom of a bottle and attaching an old webcam Harry literally had lying around in his office to the bottom of the bottle. They secured the camera inside a plastic bag to make it waterproof, then affixed the whole assembly to the body of the bottle and put water in it. Then they recorded Harry taking a drink, viewed from the unique vantage point of being *inside* the bottle.

Harry has kept the digital still shot from that first moment. Not only was it shrewd and disruptive thinking, it also happened to lead to a breakthrough. From those humble beginnings, Continuum's informal study identified three distinct patterns of drinking from containers: the suck, the pour, and the pull. Identifying these distinct drinking modes revolutionized the way Tetra Pak thinks about what it's trying to do when it designs packaging. It turns out the company doesn't want to merely package, preserve, and deliver liquid. Instead the company also has the task of accommodating your preferred mode of drinking: suck, pour, or pull.

It seems like a small thing, but it took seven years from the discovery of the three basic modes of drinking before the first improved packaging rolled out of Tetra Pak's commercial packaging machines, which are installed all around the world. Why? Because while the insight was rapid, the discovery of the modes of drinking was only a first step in what is ultimately a significant engineering problem: how to design a package that could support the suck, the pour, and the pull, using materials that could be processed on Tetra Pak's existing manufacturing equipment. Continuum and Tetra Pak both understood that the surest way to disrupt the product for the long run was to do so without disrupting the sunk capital investment of Tetra Pak's clients. Rather than look at that existing equipment as a barrier, they had to look at it as an essentially free tool.

Using Continuum's existing resources to rapidly prototype hundreds of alternative packages as quickly as designers could imagine them, the two companies worked together to do consumer tests of the best new designs that would work on Tetra Pak's essentially free existing equipment. The result was the DreamCap, successfully tested in Saudi Arabia in 2011 and released worldwide in 2012 with the eager support of dozens of Tetra Pak clients, including Gatorade.

This process created a self-disrupting product revolution accomplished with a minimum of pain to Tetra Pak's clients, and all using existing equipment—essentially free tools—where possible to deliver a significantly improved end-customer experience. All because Harry had a webcam lying around and because he was willing to use it and other essentially free tools to ask and answer a simple question.

The digital disruptor's mindset leads disruptors to see the world differently. Everywhere that the rest of us see intractable problems, digital disruptors see a myriad of free tools that they confidently assume will help them overcome those problems. The disruptor's mind gravitates to whatever mix of totally free, nearly free, and essentially free tools will most rapidly get the job done. Digital disruptors then accelerate a cycle of free things by offering even more free tools and nearly free tools to their customers. Entwined in this cycle of free things, digital disruptors must then turn to the explosive potential bound up in something we call digital platforms—a structural component of the digitally disruptive future we'll define and exploit next.

4

Digital Disruptors
Exploit Digital Platforms

Digital disruptors see free tools everywhere they look. They use those tools to develop better product experiences. Then they exploit a key structural component of the digitally disruptive era—digital platforms—to deliver those experiences. Digital platforms enable them to deploy new products rapidly and to create and maintain digital customer relationships. They will be as crucial to your business in the coming century as railways, highways, and airways were to business in the last century.

Charles Teague joined Allaire Corporation in 1995. Allaire was the creator of ColdFusion, one of the first database-driven web-content servers. Charles joined the company in its first year and had a front-row seat for the explosion of web content and web commerce that followed, rising to the role of director of engineering.

Did this make him a tech-head? Yes. Was he a digital disruptor? Not yet.

Allaire was purchased by one of its competitors, Macromedia, in 2001. Charles left to co-found a company called Onfolio, producer of a kind of personal web research assistant. Then Microsoft bought Onfolio.

Tech startup guy? Yes. Bought out by massive technology company? Yes. Digital disruptor? Not yet.

After leaving Microsoft, Charles landed at General Catalyst, an influential venture capital firm. As technologist-in-residence, Charles was an insider on investments in up-and-coming technologies like online video, app development, and cloud computing, long before these were household words.

Venture capitalist? Yes. Digital disruptor? Not yet.

Venture capitalists, startup founders, and tech-heads abound. But a digital disruptor has a unique mindset that leads him or her to behave differently. That's what Charles did next: He and some friends developed an app and gave it away on a digital platform for free.

His iPhone app, Lose It!, rapidly shot to the top of the iPhone Health & Fitness category, attaining a 4.5 star rating from more than 300,000 reviewers. This tidy little app has, since late 2008, offered people a much-needed benefit: weight loss. It's simple: users merely log all the calories they consume and see how that affects their long-term weight. Logging calories is not disruptive, it's traditional. You can do it on paper if you want to, and there were plenty of websites that did it, even in 2008. But Charles and his associates realized right away that the iPhone was the ideal calorie tracking *platform*, one that its target customers were actively building their lives on. The iPhone platform—the hardware and software experience—was always with them, its apps were one or two finger motions away, and it gave customers powerful remote access to nutrition and personal history databases stored in the cloud. Nearly four years later, Lose It! has reached more than ten million customers using the app on iPhones, iPads, Android phones and tablets, and on the web.

This is *not* the same story we heard with the dot-com startups that were the focus of so much *Fast Company* ink in the late 1990s. While those whiz kids *seemed* similar to Charles, Charles and his collaborators on the Lose It! app are different in a way that all wannabe digital disruptors should learn from: By establishing themselves firmly on this new frontier called the digital platform, they have made themselves essential to the well-being of millions.

All without much investment. FitNow, Charles's small company behind Lose It!, waited four years before taking on a small Series A round of financing. In fact, FitNow does all that it does with just eight employees. Charles explains that he wants to "stay small and not get too far ahead of our skis. We're eight people now, but we're done growing for the time being."

Instead of escalating costs in hopes of someday escalating benefits, Charles looks at it the other way around: How can I escalate benefits delivered without actually raising costs? Without the burden of tending to investors and a burgeoning HR organization, Charles and his company can focus on customers because the platform on which they have built their business gives them rapid and unfettered access to millions of them. So far it's working. As he says, "People look at what we're doing and can't believe it's so few people. They say, 'That's fifty people for ten years for us to do what you're doing.'"

I am not here to preach that the company of the future consists of only eight people. You can disrupt from within a larger company. But I am here to introduce to you the mindset of a digital disruptor so that you can crawl inside his brain, because it is only by consciously adopting that digital platform-exploiting mindset that you will be able to replicate Charles's success.

Let's examine what successful platform-exploiting disruption is—and what it isn't.

A platform is only as powerful as the digital bridge it builds to the customer. It used to be that large retail stores bragged of having 20 million customers, and that is indeed a powerful analog relationship. But those customers only came to the store, on average, two or three times a year. In a digital era, companies like Gilt Groupe can get millions of customers to visit the site or use an app two or three times *a day*. This changes the target customer metrics tremendously, from a few transactions per year or quarter to the minutes of engagement per day that an app can achieve.[1] This new metric becomes a perpetual customer relationship, one that digital disruptors see as the most desirable thing in the world; they organize their entire business to tap those platforms most likely to generate the most minutes of engagement per day from the most people.

Thanks to digital platforms, digital relationships become simultaneously more important and more frictionless, a combination that is ideal for rapid innovation. In Charles's case, the apps and the website represent a digital bridge over which he and his team can deliver improved features and experiences. Over that same bridge, customers can tell him whether they like what he has done and what else they want him and his team to do. All he has to do is develop, deliver, listen, and repeat. It's an achingly simple model, and thanks to the availability of digital platforms, people like Charles exploit it so fully that it becomes as comfortable as their own skin.

This approach depends on another thing the digital disruptor mindset holds dear: measurement. Measurement as a business discipline is not new. But today, thanks to tools built into the digital platform that Charles exploits to reach his millions of customers, he has real-time insight into what his customers do and what they want.

Just asking customers for feedback won't lead to the breakthrough disruptions at breakneck speeds that digital disruption requires, because customers don't always know what they want. Charles and other disruptors instead derive their feedback from the digital platform itself, allowing them to test ideas faster than most companies can agree on what food to order for a so-called brainstorming offsite. That rapid testing leads to rapid generation of new ideas which can then be tested right away. But what ideas do you start the test-and-respond cycle with? Charles puts it this way: "We think about what we would call user-demanded features. Actually, it's a bit of prospective thinking on our part. We have theories about this or that thing, then we put these features in and see how people take to them." As he puts it, "Your job is to pick what you can fix for [users]. But you also have to set aside a substantial piece of your budget to work on things people aren't going to ask you for."

To do this right, digital disruptors have to innovate continually, identifying specific improvements they want to offer customers to see how they will respond, knowing that not everything will work. Yes, digital disruptors will fail, usually more often than they will succeed. But because they use free tools in the process—and because they exploit digital platforms that require almost no investment and provide such immediate feedback—failure becomes a cheap teacher.

For example, Charles and his team created a substantial upgrade for Lose It! in which they added a social dimension to the app. "It turns out that if you look at weight loss tracking as the most foundational, then you next have to add peer support. If you look at the industry, Weight Watchers and so on, you have to let users engage with one another. Only we can do it digitally—that's the approach we wanted to take, rather than meetups." Appropriate thinking for a digital disruptor.

The upgrade allowed users to invite their friends, via Facebook, to join them on Lose It!, where they could share goals and, hopefully, triumphs. It didn't go so well. "People end up using the thing differently than you anticipated they would use it. We really assumed that losing weight is a personal thing, [that] you would rather bring a set of friends with you. Turns out, a lot of our users come by themselves and would rather meet someone they don't know."

Once the company saw its own users posting their email addresses on public discussion boards so that other Lose It! users could friend them in the app, Charles understood they had gotten this wrong. Because the company bases its entire business on a digital platform, it is optimized to respond quickly. The team was able to retool the upgrade so that users could search for other users based on weight-loss goals, specific diets, or other criteria. The failed upgrade became a success, because Charles and his colleagues treated failure as feedback.

An obsession with digital relationships, a passion for measuring results, and a fondness for rapid innovation cycles in which failure is viewed as cheap feedback—these are traits that make Charles and his team digital disruptors. But every single one of these traits depends on a digital platform for its fullest and fastest expression. If these traits describe how digital disruptors approach business, it is the digital platform that maximizes the power of that approach.

How did we get to a world where eight people could upend an industry? If you're not bothered by this question, you should be. Even if you're in a large company, you should be wondering if you can adopt the mindset and traits of a digital disruptor. You can, thanks to a new digital structure that is now solidly in place: the *digital platform*. Digital platforms make scale irrelevant and cut barriers to entry to nearly nothing. They make digital disruption possible for anyone in any company, large or small.

For decades the prevailing wisdom has been that a company had to grow in size in order to achieve economies of scale. But today many of the economies of scale that matter most *don't have to reside in the company* for the company to benefit from them. They can instead be attributes of a digital platform that a company exploits. In the case of FitNow, the platforms the company depends on—and exploits to scale—include Apple iOS, Google Android, and the web.

These platforms are fundamental to the success of all digital disruptors. But disruptors *exploit* platforms, they don't have to *create* them. Conversely, the platform creators succeed by enabling disruption, but they are not necessarily disruptors themselves. Apple has a knack for upending traditional businesses, and the company's spectacular track record of introducing digitally disruptive technology is hard to match. But nothing that Apple has developed has come at low cost or with quick turnaround. The same is true for Google, Microsoft, Facebook, and Amazon, which together with Apple, form the list of the major platforms competing for digital supremacy. And while all of these are digital powerhouses, they do not have to be digital disruptors themselves.

Instead, they are digital disruption *enablers*, each of them having created one or more platforms in the lives of consumers that are central to their businesses. A platform is a digital foundation on which companies and customers connect to each other with as close to zero friction as possible. Google is an archetypal platform creator. Google's platforms—including all the flavors of the Android operating environment for mobile phones, its Chrome browser, Gmail, Google Docs, and

YouTube—are designed to be as open as statutory law and the laws of consumer friction will allow. For example, anyone can upload a video to YouTube. The only restrictions in places like YouTube or Android Market are those that reduce consumer uncertainty—a deadly form of friction. YouTube features consumer ratings and comments, shows the number of views, and includes a button to report inappropriate content; these are tools for alerting the user community about where the heat is while also enabling the community to help enforce standards. The only friction Google wants left in these platforms is the friction necessary to reduce other, more deleterious frictional components.

Why so open? No company would voluntarily create such openness if it didn't have to. The platforms created by Google and Facebook are among the most open anywhere. Why? Because their open platforms draw digital disruptors to them, multiplying the reach and power of those platforms.

More platforms are coming; technology companies have caught on to their value. For example, Microsoft started selling the Kinect camera for Xbox 360—a crucial tool in Microsoft's future platform plans—on November 2, 2010. By November 7, Gizmodo reported that someone had already created an open source Kinect driver for the PC.[2] Microsoft's initial response—as dictated by lawyers, who are typically not a good source of digitally disruptive ideas—was to issue a statement threatening possible legal action.

A day later, whether motivated by the negative attention it received from its first statement or by an awareness that openness is a good thing, Microsoft issued a statement saying it didn't consider the open source driver a hack and would not pursue legal action.[3] In other words, "The door is open, come on in."

Microsoft later revealed that it had specifically designed the USB connector on the Kinect without any encryption or proprietary pin scheme so that the output from the camera could be useful in a wide variety of potential contexts. The company then went on to release an SDK in 2011 that allowed academic and personal development of Kinect-fueled experiences, followed in February 2012 by a version for corporate use. And yes, the SDK is free.

Platform providers understand that their core value depends on their ability to encourage as many interactions and transactions as possible over their platforms. It's happening at Facebook, it's happening at Amazon, and it's even happening at Apple, where the company continues to reevaluate its monastic practices in favor of more openness. The door to this kind of openness is still less than halfway open at Apple, but the significant weight of digital disruption being applied to the door will eventually blow it wide open until there is a near-zero friction policy in effect at every one of these major platforms.

No friction in the digital platform means that anyone can play. Large or small. And that's how the rest of us will be able to realize our digitally disruptive potential.

———

For digital disruption to work, thousands (and eventually millions) of people have to try it. It is out of this relentless and accelerating competition that the dramatic benefits of digital disruption will emerge. There are already hundreds of thousands of these people hard at work. Without the digital platforms that provide the promise of possible access and success, the many thousands eager to participate in digital disruption would have nowhere near the motivation required to upend markets and remake industries. The lesson of Charles Teague and Lose It! is that these digital platforms really do offer unprecedented access to customers, if you exploit those digital platforms to:

- Build digital bridges to your customers.
- Measure early and often.
- Iterate quickly based on feedback.

See anything on this list that only startups or eight-person companies can do? No. In fact, because digital platforms are available to everyone, they are perfectly suited for large companies to exploit as well. In many cases, a large company has more resources, more expertise, and more potential sources of ideas worth testing than a small startup does. What a large company typically lacks is a digitally disruptive mindset.

But there's nothing stopping a large company, even one with a very analog business, from adopting that mindset. Let's look at an example. Consider Vestas, a Danish company vying to become a leader in the wind turbine business. Having won contracts to deploy hundreds of wind turbines in wind farms in countries like Belgium, the UK, and Sweden, Vestas is growing nicely towards its goals of supporting countries interested in renewable sources of energy.

It's a difficult business that can get downright nasty at times because of the politics involved in energy policy. Communities don't always want massive wind turbines in their midst and the current energy producers in many markets would rather not face the competition new providers bring. To overcome this, a company like Vestas has to maximize every opportunity to keep costs down while overdelivering on the value its turbines provide. They do this in ways you'd expect, like transporting the 55-meter-long turbine blades in the most economical ways possible.

How could a company like Vestas exploit digital platforms?

As it turns out, these turbines are loaded with sensors that can track any kind of stress to ensure the blades are turning safely. The turbine towers and blades can sense the direction and velocity of incoming wind so that the blades can be angled into the wind to maximize energy generation. This investment in sensors creates the ideal conditions for collecting, processing, and communicating that data back to the operators who are most concerned with the turbine's success. But if Vestas and its customers are smart, they will use those sensors to create digital relationships with other people outside of the control room.

Imagine that a week's worth of sensor readings shows that the turbine is performing at lower cost or greater efficiency than planned. That information ought to be available to the local community that installed the turbine, helping to boost their confidence in the massive wind machine that was built in their backyards. Or imagine that wind conditions become unstable and sensors indicate that the turbines have to be locked down to ensure their integrity and protect the adjacent community. A smart turbine operator would be happy to share this information with the community, to let citizens know that the operator is adhering to safety standards and keeping watchful care over the town.

In an era of digital disruption, the way to share this information is not through the occasional press release, but through digital platforms that create a cheap, instantaneous, and reassuring relationship with citizens, activists, and politicians. An app built for Apple devices or even a Facebook page that community members can "Like" would establish that immediate digital bridge with facility operators. Sensors could pipe certain types of information directly to the app or Facebook page, providing real-time insight into the energy generated by the wind. Vestas could encourage local schoolteachers to teach the children in the community how to check the data, helping aspiring engineers in local high school classes to download and incorporate the data into their schoolwork, analyzing the cost of wind power versus other sources. That fearless future is obvious to a digital disruptor. It is not, however, the way today's energy sector works, nor the way activists and politicians prefer to operate. All the more reason to disrupt them, too. Much of their power and influence should be redirected into the hands of the local community anyway.

By offering such a software solution to local installations, a company like Vestas would be using essentially free tools—the sensors already built into its turbines—and exploiting digital platforms to change the relationship the company has with its customers and the relationship its customers have with their constituents. With that digital relationship in place, both Vestas and its customers could then use that digital channel to measure not only product efficiency but customer satisfaction. Vestas would be in a powerful position to inform each of its customers how it is performing compared to aggregate measurements from Vestas's other customers. That would allow those customers to then iterate based on that rapid, digital feedback to make improvements in the turbine operation as well community relations.

All because easily exploited digital platforms provide a new avenue for connecting with and learning from digital customers.

————

Whether you're an eight-person company or a manufacturer of massive industrial equipment, a digital mindset opens you to new ways to exploit the rising digital platforms that will soon serve as the foundations for our daily experiences. How we schedule a doctor's appointment and review our blood test results, how we estimate when the children's school bus will arrive at our bus stop, how we track the long-term strength of our most personal relationships: All of these things can be improved at low cost and with dramatic effect, all depending on the exploitation of digital platforms.

If it sounds like there's a lot of work ahead of those of us who want to be digital disruptors, there is. However, there's one area where you need not invest a single speck of energy. And that's in persuading consumers to join the digital disruption. Because as you'll see in the next chapter, consumers are already there, waiting for you to join them.

5

Digital Consumers Want to Fulfill Their Needs

igital consumers are not a new type of animal. But as digitally empowered creatures, they are equipped with more ways to meet their fundamental needs more rapidly than ever before. The only way to keep up with them is to meet them on their terms, to serve those fundamental needs more fully than before. But what *are* their fundamental needs? It turns out that Maslow's famous hierarchy of needs is a poor guide. I propose a new model of fundamental human needs.[1] To become a digital disruptor, you have to become obsessed with finding more ways to meet more consumer needs more quickly than before.

————

In early 2011, around the one-year anniversary of the iPad, we gathered a group of clients in New York for a private dinner. Joining me were clients from some of the largest technology companies and most influential media firms on the planet. It was a rare occasion to get them out of their individual offices and have them share their experiences of dealing with digital disruption—which, of course, they only would do on neutral turf, in the company of others like them.

To get the ball rolling, I came with a couple of questions at the ready to stimulate discussion. I explained that we'd run the evening in the style of the legendary Algonquin Round Table: I would arbitrarily offer points to whoever said anything brilliant, witty, or otherwise impactful along the way. I then tossed out what turned out to be the conversational equivalent of a Molotov cocktail.

"Are consumers fundamentally different today than they were before all of this digital disruption?"

What ensued was a powerful and passionate discussion on both sides of the debate. I was compelled to give out points to many people arguing for each side. Because my role was host, I did not impose my own view on the discussion, but that didn't stop me from fanning the flames on both sides of the issue whenever possible.

The clients have long since gone home and the food is just a pleasant memory, but the question persists: Are consumers fundamentally different today?

Here's the answer: Human beings are the same as they have always been. They have not changed—they want the same things they have always wanted. So how is it that I can promise the kinds of dramatic changes that digital disruption will bring? Because what has changed is consumers' ability to *get* what they want. This has led them to expect that their needs can and should be met—more often and more completely than ever before in human history.

So while people have not fundamentally changed, the way they act out their fundamental drives and urges has changed. This shift isn't new. It has been taking place gradually over the past two hundred years, in the wake of the movement toward democracy and the Industrial Revolution, but the arrival of the digital era has sped up the change dramatically.

Put these unchanged people in a dramatically more inviting environment and you get what appears to be a fundamentally altered consumer, one you can only see clearly if you have the digital disruptor's mindset. Who is this new customer? The digitally empowered consumer. It is this consumer you must harness. Either that or stand back while they sprint ahead of you.

———

Remember 1999? The big digital question was who would win the battle between AOL, Netscape, and Microsoft Internet Explorer. There was no Facebook or YouTube. Google had just started up and failed to sell itself to Excite for $1 million. Even Napster, which would eventually rewrite the rules of the music industry, had been operating for only a few months and college students had yet to discover and exploit it.

It was in that year that Forrester asked me to deliver the keynote speech at a Forrester Forum, our big client event. As an analyst at Forrester, my job had been to pore over massive amounts of consumer survey data from Forrester's Consumer Technographics research. In doing so, I could see a very clear shift ahead. The future was going to be different from the past in ways that we could anticipate and prepare for. My speech, "Meet the Digital Consumers," was designed to make everyone aware that digitally-empowered consumers would be uniquely important and market-shaping. At the time, this idea was controversial and presumptuous.

To really convince an audience, we had to find data about the future consumer before that consumer actually existed. So we looked into a crystal ball: We surveyed 8,500 online youth between the ages of sixteen and twenty-two. These kids didn't have any of the longstanding consumer habits or behaviors that tied the rest of us down. Whatever they embraced quickly could reasonably be held up as the future—either because those people would grow up to become the future or because what they did would be so compelling the rest of us would imitate them.

In fact, both of these shifts ended up happening. In my speech in 1999, I introduced that audience to the digital consumer in the persona of Billy, a seventeen-year-old boy. Digital consumers like him were still relatively unknown animals, but the data allowed me to show that they would soon roam the economy in large herds. We knew his behavior was different because, unlike most older consumers, Billy had already demonstrated sophisticated online behaviors like maintaining multiple email accounts and using many different computers in the same day to access the internet. I couldn't say he used Facebook more than email, and I couldn't say that he spent hours a day on his iPhone, because none of those things existed yet and wouldn't for years. But with the few tools he had available, he went digital crazy.

I summarized the effect of Billy and his peers with a single statement: *When people adopt technology, they do old things in new ways. When people internalize technology, they find new things to do.*

It was as straightforward a way as I could find to express how Billy and his cohort would be the undoing of traditional business. They wouldn't just use digital technology to improve on old things. They would—powered by technology—be open to entirely new experiences. And those experiences, when unleashed, would force everything else to change.

Digital consumers did, indeed, change the world, not by becoming a new breed but by using digital technology to maximize their own satisfaction. The result is that today there are more than one billion regular users of Facebook.[2] Forty-eight hours of video are uploaded to YouTube every minute, which comes out to eight years' worth of video uploaded every twenty-four hours.[3]

To help you keep this digital consumer foremost in your mind, I want to put a face up on your mental bulletin board. But don't imagine Billy. Instead, imagine Colonel Steve Austin, the title character in the 1970s TV show *The Six Million Dollar Man*. The conceit of this show was simple: Amplified by technology, this one human being was better, stronger, and faster than everyone else. He was still human, he was just an amplified, exaggerated human.

I see elements of the Six Million Dollar Man in all the digital consumers I have studied since that speech in 1999. These are all people who are digitally enhanced—bionic, if you will, achieving feats of superhuman strength and intelligence.

———

If digital consumers are enhanced humans, then keeping up with their digital power will require, first, understanding why humans do what they do in the first place. Then we will be able to project just how differently they will behave once they are digitally enabled.

If I were to ask you why people behave the way they do, you might be tempted to construct a reply based on Maslow's hierarchy of needs. That would make sense because it's what you were taught in Psych 101 and everybody else believes it, too. So get ready, because I am going to eviscerate Maslow's hierarchy. I know you didn't pick up this book to learn more about fundamental human psychology, but we have to go there now, because it matters in your business planning. If you move forward in any aspect of your business planning while still retaining the misleading understanding of human psychology suggested by Maslow's hierarchy, you will fail to anticipate the rapidly growing expectations of your customers.

Abraham Maslow developed his famous hierarchy in 1943 by studying people he felt were exemplary, such as Eleanor Roosevelt and Albert Einstein, as well as college students at elite institutions. His goal was laudable. He thought that by looking closely at the people who were at the pinnacle of the social order he could help everyone else emulate them and thus avoid the follies of the lower classes. Thanks to his study of elite individuals, Maslow proposed his famous explanation for how our needs motivate us. Some of the things he concluded are true, most are not.

Maslow's most enduring contribution to the study of human needs— and the only one that I won't refute—is that human needs are shared by the entire race, regardless of one's location on the map, in history, or in the landscape of human culture. Whether you realize it or not, all product development is done under the assumption that needs are general; if they weren't, how could you design something like mobile speakers without faith that the needs of the people you interact with will be common to many other consumers?

But Maslow moved from his idea of universal needs to the claim that our shared needs are hierarchical. Maslow did not include a pyramid in his original study, but the pyramid later came to embody Maslow's philosophy. Basically, in Maslow's view, we all start at the bottom of the pyramid, fulfilling basic physiological needs, and only progress to satisfying higher-order needs once we have a stable source for fulfilling lower-order needs (see Figure 5-1).[4] Thus, adapting Maslow, psychiatrists and self-help gurus talk about how we are likely to "revert" to lower levels of need when we are frustrated with our inability to fulfill higher-order needs.

Figure 5-1: Maslow's Hierarchy of Needs

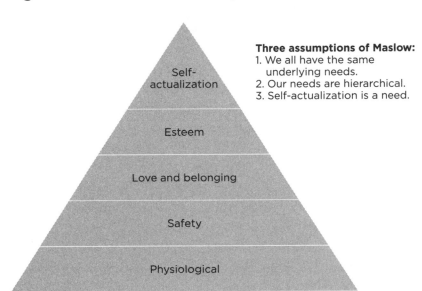

Three assumptions of Maslow:
1. We all have the same underlying needs.
2. Our needs are hierarchical.
3. Self-actualization is a need.

Source: A.H. Maslow, "A Theory of Human Motivation," *Psychological Review*, 50, pp 370-398

At the top of his pyramid, Maslow placed his most untenable claim, that self-actualization is a need. This one clearly comes from the sample that Maslow studied—remember, these are Yale and Harvard grads— leading him to the elitist claim that only people who have climbed his ladder can achieve the peaceful state of self-actualization. Product marketers often tie their products to this mythical state—Audi once pitched its A8 as embodying "the art of perfection." Misled by Maslow, the Audi ad crew imagined that a vehicle that attains the pinnacle of the principles of design and engineering is obviously the ideal companion for a self-actualized individual.

However, in the 1980s a Chilean academic, Manfred Max-Neef, finally challenged the Maslow fan club. While he accepted Maslow's assertion that humans share a common set of fundamental needs, he went on to explain that our needs are nowhere near as orderly as Maslow suggested.[5] A moment of honest introspection will reveal that this is true: that your fundamental needs are at odds with each other, each vying for priority depending on a complex mix of how long it has been since each has been fulfilled and what your current opportunity for need fulfillment is. In fact, brain science now shows that *there is no central authority in the brain making executive decisions.*[6] As a result, people don't behave in rational and ordered ways. Instead, the multiple paths that the brain employs to manage multiple inputs and direct multiple outputs compete with one other, ensuring that the few rational priorities people possess shift continuously.

The brain is governed by regionalized functions that act independently of one another. Thanks to technologies like functional MRI, scientists have learned that the brain processes its vast array of inputs in multiple, overlapping systems that behave according to their own rules of regulation, often without consulting one another. Furthermore, the body can play an active role in brain function by delivering hormones that alter the way regions of the brain perform their functions. This interplay leads us to perceive ourselves as subject to various whims and changes of mood.

So forget Maslow's pyramid, since it doesn't help us to understand how digital consumers behave or how to harness their power. To see what this means in practice, visit a Best Buy and watch a tech geek stand torn between the PCs, the game consoles, and the connected TVs in a smorgasbord of competitive need fulfillment.

Because needs compete, they have a tendency to manifest themselves urgently in response to circumstances—either threats or opportunities. For example, a married man attending a large convention in Las Vegas may feel satisfied by the long-distance companionship of his wife miles away until an attractive alternative appears next to him at the blackjack table. A savvy, artistic twentysomething who idolizes the iPad may find herself compelled to get a Kindle Fire because it helps her manage her budget more effectively while still delivering many of the values she would derive from the iPad. Because the way we experience our needs is determined by both conscious and subconscious processes, humans are no better at predicting which needs they will most want to fulfill in the future than they are at predicting the weather a week out.

Figure 5-2: The Four Fundamental Human Needs

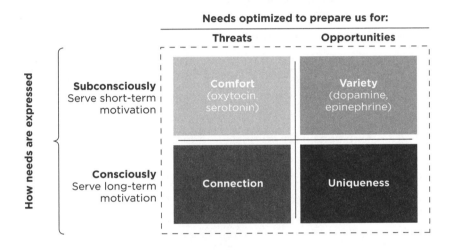

We need an alternative model. This is what I call the *four fundamental human needs model* (see Figure 5-2) and it meets stringent criteria that prior thinkers were able to ignore. It accounts for what we know about human physiology and explains how human needs affect individual behaviors, but it's still simple enough to guide digital disruptors to a better product strategy.

Need No. 1: Comfort

The most basic human need is the need for comfort. The word "comfort" encompasses many experiences and states of being, including reassurance, serenity, security, and safety. This need is characterized by a desire to remove stress and reduce complexity. The need for comfort operates mostly at a subconscious level, serving to generate short-term feelings of well-being that reduce anxiety.

Comfort asserts itself in response to threats to well-being. The human brain is designed to deal with two types of conditions: threat and opportunity. Threats are primary—the brain sets several regions on autopilot, looking for anything that might harm us. In response to threat signals, these regions flood the brain and body with unpleasant levels of hormones such as adrenaline or cortisol, encouraging the conscious mind to find a solution to the present problem, thus reducing the unpleasant hormones and restoring a state of comfort.

Comfort is the easiest of our four needs to justify biologically. It arises directly from the release and uptake of neurotransmitters such as oxytocin and serotonin, hormones that provide feelings of well-being and security. It should be easy to see how comfort has always played a role in consumer products and marketing. Consider the most successful marketing campaigns in history and you'll immediately recognize the role of comfort in building successful products and brands. From buying the world a Coke to the "Mmm Mmm Good" deliciousness of Campbell's soup, selling comfort always yields significant returns.

Need No. 2: Connection

Comfort is so fundamental a need that it spawns a sister need: a conscious desire to connect to other people for the mutual safety and security that such connections provide. Connection can be achieved on multiple levels and through a variety of interpersonal mechanisms, such as touch, conversation, shared experiences—and this is also where we explain the otherwise baffling success of FarmVille. Connection is as wired into us as our awareness of our own mortality. In fact, there is an entire academic theory, terror management theory, devoted to demonstrating that when we are primed with an awareness of our own mortality, we respond by affirming our social connections more deeply than we would otherwise.[7] This means that we'll feel more patriotic, affirm community religious and moral standards, and even judge outsiders more harshly, all as a defense against threats. Our bonds to other people—though conscious aspects of our personal experience—are motivated at a very deep, biological level.

Here again, connection sells products and services. Whether it's when a trusted celebrity hawks a brand of soda or when Facebook promises us that we can friend the world, our response is the same. We sign up to follow somebody on Twitter because we perceive that our need for connection will be met—a connection to people we already care about or to those celebrities or public figures with whom we have a one-way, parasocial relationship.

Need No. 3: Variety

While comfort and connection serve to prepare us to cope with threats to our safety and well-being, the human organism must also be prepared to seek opportunities for expansion and growth. Variety is the first of two needs that prepare us for opportunities. It is characterized by feelings of excitement and possibility, the anticipation of novelty and diversion, and positive uncertainty. Like comfort, variety operates primarily at a subconscious level, serving to stimulate the body and mind to consider new behaviors and to engage in situations that may yield positive returns for the individual.

Variety manifests itself in response to crushing sameness. Any parent who has listened to children complain that they are bored, bored, bored after only a week of summer vacation will recognize this need for stimuli that is native to the human animal. When neurological inputs repeat themselves or sustain themselves without interruption, the brain pays decreasing attention to them until they are no longer noticed or grow wearisome. That's why a back scratch eventually stops feeling good or why we can watch most movies just once—or why a teenager can listen to a new Lady Gaga song obsessively for a week and then suddenly drop it like last week's stale bread. When our minds know what's coming, they generate less enthusiasm for it, preferring instead the unexpected.

This need is moderated by chemicals like dopamine and epinephrine. One success factor in long-lasting marriages, for example, is that these couples engage in novel behaviors—visiting new restaurants or traveling to new destinations together.[8] This triggers the release of dopamine in the couple's brains, stimulating their need for variety while reinforcing the feelings of connection and romance that they feel for one another. The chemicals released when encountering new and varied experiences are so vital to healthy functioning that a body isolated in a sensory deprivation chamber for extended periods will actually generate false external experiences—in other words, hallucinations—in order to supply the brain with needed stimuli.

Variety also drives billions in consumer purchases. We need look no further than Mountain Dew, the cult of personality surrounding skateboarder Tony Hawk, or the glory days of MTV to understand how the desire for variety and novelty can be successfully fulfilled for commercial purposes. It's not just youth who desire change, however. The ubiquitous "new and improved" labels found on the latest incarnations of Tide and Crest demonstrate that the variety supplied by changing stimuli targets a clear need that consumers have, even if that need hovers mostly below the limits of consciousness.

Need No. 4: Uniqueness

Even though people want to connect to other human beings, they also want to feel unique and special in the world. Uniqueness serves as the conscious expression of a lower-level desire to prepare for possible opportunities and improvements in one's situation. A sense of uniqueness allows us to have optimistic expectations about our own chances when such opportunities arise, even when others around us struggle.

Uniqueness is a form of self-identification that confers benefits. Anyone who has survived high school knows that while having friends is important, having the right friends is even better. That's why people will go to great lengths to separate themselves from the masses through their choice of hobbies, favorite music, preferred blogs, and hair and clothing styles.

This need can motivate consumers to pay a premium. The desire to distinguish oneself from the herd is strong enough that people will pay extra for it. The truly wealthy will obviously spring for a Mercedes-Benz or a Porsche, but even someone with less cash may still desire a flashy car— often "modding" or "pimping'" it to signal his unique identity. Much of our research into technology adoption has demonstrated that status plays a role in buying things like large-screen TVs or the latest smartphones.

By now, it's clear that human needs are neither simple nor straightfor-ward. Yet we can summarize such complexity with just four distinct needs because these four can combine in infinite ways—and in response to local circumstances, they can produce the wide range of feelings, desires, and urges we feel each day. But if these needs are universal and product marketers from every industry have learned how to exploit them, why am I presenting them to you as if they matter more now?

Because they do. These fundamental needs have always been with us, but thanks to rapid consumer digitization, these needs are prominent in a way that was not possible to see before. Just imagine your grandparents, whether they were kids of the Depression or World War II. The range of options and choices they had available to them were smaller by many orders of magnitude than what you have today, whether you consider what they could eat for lunch or how they could communicate across distances or where and when they could find out what the Lone Ranger was up to. This lack of options had a natural dampening effect on their expectations, thus shifting down their brains to anticipate and plan for less fulfillment.

Today brains have shifted into overdrive. Thanks to digital, we have the ability to meet more of our needs more often and to a greater degree than our grandparents, our parents or even ourselves from just ten years ago. In fact, it's not just the case that digitally empowered consumers can meet more needs, they can meet more needs simultaneously. Buying an iPod a decade ago might have satisfied a few of your needs, but buying an iPad today satisfies many more needs, more deeply, all at once.

I attacked Maslow's hierarchy because it's embedded unconsciously in the mindset of most businesspeople. The new needs I have described should now replace Maslow's as a clear mandate for action in your day-to-day response to digital consumers. Thanks to their embrace of digital experiences, you face intense pressure to meet their fundamental needs more fully than before. Digital disruptors already think this way. Digital disruptors may not have known the names of the needs or the hormones involved in their expression, but they were already able to look at messy, conflicting, urgent human needs and begin to imagine the digital solutions they could create to satisfy multiple needs in one digital stroke. You can think this way, too, by adopting a few specific practices:

First, map product experiences to needs. Identify how your product does or does not meet the four fundamental needs. Pay close attention to the words you use when attempting this. Fun and excitement go under the need of variety, exclusivity fits under uniqueness, and so on. Do this until you've described every aspect of your product's experience and you can list the ways in which you meet each need. You will find that your product leans heavily toward one or two dominant needs and serves the other needs at a lower level, if at all.

Second, analyze how conveniently your product meets needs. For each need you believe you are meeting, rate how conveniently you help people meet that need compared with the nearest alternatives. This comparison is crucial in a digital era because, equipped with the right technology, people are always a click away from another way to meet that same need.

Third, plan to meet more needs *more conveniently*. Your product may never meet all four needs simultaneously, but you should insistently expand the number of needs you can satisfy, gradually extending into adjacent possibilities, which I'll describe in chapter 6. This task is significantly easier thanks to digital tools you can use to build digital product experiences that will enhance and expand the very nature of the product itself, as I'll explain in chapter 7.

––––

It's barely more than a year since I sat with those clients at dinner in New York to share a meal and an evening of stimulating conversation. Yet in that time, the proof of what I'm saying has accelerated beyond even my wildest imaginings. By the time you read this, Apple will already have sold more than 100 million iPads around the world. If iPad users were a country unto themselves, they would rank number twelve on the list, closing in on Mexico sometime in 2013. And we estimate that by year-end 2012, there will be nearly 42 million adults in the United States with an eReader and a likely 30 million homes globally that have at least one Kinect for Xbox 360. Compare this to Apple's original innovation, the iPod, which took two years to sell one million units. So while the smattering of devices and platforms I offer may seem disjointed and disconnected, when you add them all up, they point to the same conclusion: People are behaving differently from even their near ancestors, even if they share the same fundamental needs that have preserved the species since the dawn of time.

This is the final chapter in the section on adopting a digital disruptor's mindset. A digital disruptor thinks like this and therefore intuitively understands what other digital consumers want. This is different from just tapping into people's mobile lifestyles or merely seeking digital channel efficiencies. Instead, when you understand the accelerated power of the digital consumer, you tap into human brains operating at a more powerful level than ever before. Stimulated by an environment that can give millions of them more choices than humans in any prior era had a right to expect, today's brains—though built on the same blueprint that made Homo sapiens domesticate fire and invent the wheel—are hungrily calculating, connecting, and anticipating all the things that you are about to create for them. And brains in that state will test and ultimately embrace those disruptive innovations, provided they meet as many needs as conveniently as possible. Otherwise, they'll move on, because digitally empowered brains have important work to do.

Now that you have a digital disruptor's mindset, you see what a digital disruptor sees. You see the free tools you can use, the digital platforms you must exploit, and the accelerated digital consumers you have to serve. But this insight is only the beginning. For it to save you and your company, you can—you must—behave like a digital disruptor.

PART 3

Behave Like a Digital Disruptor

6

Generate More Ideas More Quickly

Faced with digital disruption on all sides, you now have to generate more innovative ideas than ever before, more quickly than before. You will do that by employing a technique called *innovating the adjacent possible*. This means rapidly identifying a list of the *next* things your customers want and quickly giving them the few that are easiest for you to deliver. In this model, we do not predict the future of our product. We start with the next possible thing our customer needs and let the future find us.

You are the case study in this chapter. Imagine that I have come to spend a day with your team to help you with a very difficult question: How in the world can our team—composed of mere humans—generate one hundred times more idea power than we generated last year?

It's an unsettling but common question. Recently, I was on the phone with a VP responsible for product innovation at a large membership-based organization. We were evaluating whether it was worth it for her to bring me in for a workshop with her team. I gave her the thirty-minute version of everything you've read so far, and even though we were on the phone, I could tell she was nodding. She got it. But her initial excitement was immediately tempered by two quick realizations:

1. My people already think they know how to innovate.
2. But they're doing it wrong.

She didn't speak in a numbered list, I added that. And I did so because the sentence she uttered as a single phrase actually contains two different barriers: lack of knowledge and incorrect action. If people think they already know how to generate new and innovative ideas, they won't be willing to listen to what I'm about to share with you. But it's worse than that. Because by confidently proceeding down the wrong path, they will actually harm the company by generating so-called innovative ideas that not only won't lead to digitally disruptive outcomes, but will suck up all the leadership attention, energy, and resources that could have been spent on digital disruption.

As a result, before I could work with her to help her team generate more ideas, more quickly than before, I would first have to teach them what innovation isn't. It boils down to a false dichotomy that most companies have bought into, namely, the difference between incremental and ideal innovation.

Incremental innovators are usually the people tasked with making things happen, and they pride themselves on being pragmatic and focused. They reject ideas that don't connect to today's products, today's processes, and today's customers. They want proof that a thing can be done before they will sign up to do it, they reject concepts that they can't test with target customers, and they obsess about things like whether the OK button on the app should be light or dark blue. They figure that if you can't see what end state you're headed toward, you shouldn't step off in that direction. These people are important to your company's day-to-day success and you need them. But when it comes to generating more ideas, more quickly, they are a disaster.

Ideal innovators, on the other hand, often reside in marketing, product strategy, business development, or, in a worst-case scenario, the C-suite! These people like to talk about "blue-sky" or "greenfield" opportunities. They talk endlessly of changing the paradigm, breaking down barriers, and evolving the mindset. They don't want to be shackled to existing products and processes. They figure that there's a perfect—an ideal—version of your product out there and all you have to do is generate a powerful enough vision of what that product is and then draw a straight line between where you are today and where you need to be and you'll have made the next iPad. I love these people because they are fun to spend a day with. But when it comes to disruptive innovation, they are just as useless as the incremental innovators.

This dichotomy lay at the heart of my client's dilemma. She had people in the company who were busying themselves generating incremental ideas. "Our members like our travel promotions," she told me, "so when I ask for innovative ideas, the team says, 'Let's add cruises!'" Because she caught on quickly to the idea of digital disruption, she realized that these people weren't doing it. But on the other side, she had the opposite problem. "We have executives who are saying, 'Let's get into a completely different business, maybe even targeting a different customer, because our current business is slowing down.'"

Instead, she needed to adopt a different way of seeking ideas called *innovating the adjacent possible*. Once we discussed it, she saw it would break the logjam, but only if she could get people to cast aside both incremental and ideal innovation. But that's tricky, because most people will think there are no other alternatives. As she put it, "If I tell people we need to innovate, they'll all think they're already doing it. But they're doing it wrong."

No offense intended, but you're probably doing it wrong, too. Or, you were doing it just fine in the 1980s, the 1990s, and even the 2000s. But now that digital disruption has arrived, what was once right is now wrong.

Jawbone is an unusual name for a product of any kind, but especially when applied to the sophisticated, premium products that Jawbone makes. At prices ranging from $99 to $139, Jawbone Bluetooth headsets cost three to four times as much as the Plantronics Bluetooth headset that is the current bestseller on Amazon. First introduced in 2006, Jawbone's Bluetooth headset was a unique entry into a marketplace that was quickly filling up with other brands such as Plantronics and Motorola. Jawbone had to set itself apart from the very beginning, which it did by regularly enhancing the product—looking for adjacent consumer benefits to deliver, even if it meant pushing technological limits.

Travis Bogard, the VP of product management and strategy at Jawbone, explains, "Sometimes it requires innovation, like in the electronics we use in our headsets—we developed flexible circuit boards which allow for the headsets to conform to the roundness of a user's face. Other headsets use a traditional, flat computer board that may feel awkward when worn whereas Jawbone headsets focus on wearability and design."

In another adjacent improvement, Jawbone then reevaluated the boxes the products ship in. "We could use the same see-through plastic packaging that everybody uses, but it's flimsy and doesn't meet the standards of the premium product we offer. Yet we want it to be recyclable like the flimsy stuff. So we actually had to work with companies to invent a new process to create a premium package that was both strong and clear, while also achieving the same level of recyclability of the flimsier plastic."

This sounds like traditional innovation, but looking deeper, you see that it's a pattern of seeking one adjacent possibility after another, refining and improving the product by moving through adjacency after adjacency. The result was a line of Bluetooth headsets that were meticulously refined to anticipate and address the needs of customers. But moving from adjacency to adjacency doesn't only lead to refinements of existing products. Occasionally, when it is done right, it can lead to discontinuous yet still adjacent leaps.

That's what happened when Jawbone looked ahead and realized the premium Bluetooth headset market would eventually mature. The company needed to come up with the next thing. So Jawbone released a portable speaker.

Ask anyone in the consumer electronics business what category to invest in, and they'll tell you to avoid getting into speakers. The "last mile" (or few inches) of the audio business is clogged with barely differentiated commodity products that do not inspire users. There are specific niches—noise-canceling headphones, for example, or Bose SoundWave home theater equipment—where there is some money to be made, but only with high risks, significant marketing effort, strong distribution relationships, and patience.

Portable speakers are not one of those niches. Or at least they weren't, until Jawbone made them one. Before Jawbone, portable speakers were either cabled, dime-a-dozen cheapies with a tinny taint or wireless upscale affairs designed for occasional use by people who wanted to have outdoor parties without looking for a place to plug speakers in. But even solid and effective Bluetooth speakers from Logitech or Creative don't cost more than $150. Because no one would pay more than that for portable speakers, right?

To be fair, maybe it was outlandish for Jawbone to charge $199 for a speaker so small you can hold it in your hand. After all, how often do you really find yourself wishing you could pump out deep bass from your mobile phone? A couple of times a month, maybe.

That's not how the creators of Jambox saw it, however. Instead of asking, "Can we make a portable speaker we can sell?" the company asked, "What would people do if we gave them the ability to experience all of the content on their smartphone with uncompromised audio quality?" That is, what if instead of a portable speaker, the company created a *mobile* speaker. The difference in the question—and in the way Jawbone answered the question—is what accounts for why Jawbone's little speaker-that-could quickly became not only a bestseller in the category, but is essentially the definition of a new category of mobile audio device.

Jawbone's Jambox brought premium sound to a form factor that was easy to charge, connect, and carry. This little speaker not only sounded better than the portable speakers that came before it, it looked better, making what could be a cumbersome accessory into a fashionable one. And because each customer experience detail the company learned from the Jawbone headsets was carried over into this adjacent space, the Jambox experience was significantly more satisfying than other speakers. It even incorporated speakerphone capabilities to add depth to conference calls. Why? Because Jambox was designed to fit into your life as an aid to your mobile lifestyle, rather than just a way to get louder sound on the go. It was the *next* thing Jawbone's mobile customers needed, even if they didn't know it before they saw it.

Jawbone succeeded in this effort the same way the company succeeded in its first products: by innovating in the direction of its customers' needs. A focus on consumer needs opens up more possibilities—more ideas—for serving customers, to be sure. But the technique for identifying and evaluating those ideas is not obvious (or more people would do it). What Jawbone does—and what you need to do—is to innovate the adjacent possible.[1]

———

Innovating adjacent possibilities is a customer-focused discipline for rapidly generating many more product and service ideas than you can generate by merely looking at your current products and wondering what else you could do.

The term "adjacent possible" comes from evolutionary biology. Evolutionary biologist Stuart Kauffman pointed out that a complex evolutionary achievement like the eye is not the result of nature plotting a linear course from blindness to vision. Instead, vision happens as the result of nature experimenting with a large number of simultaneous adaptations which all start out as adjacent possibilities. Some of them, usually only a handful, eventually become landmark achievements. There's no need to know the ultimate outcome or even plan how to get there. Instead, imagine a blind prehistoric creature standing in a circle that represents its current capacity and capabilities. In response to adjacent openings in its environment, the organism in question will experiment evolutionarily with new abilities—new possibilities.

By Kauffman's definition, an adjacent possibility is a stable next stage in evolution or innovation that serves as a segue to the next adjacent possibility and the one after it. These adjacencies are usually not linear, or even obvious. Importantly, because the organism is experimenting with multiple adjacencies simultaneously, many of the greatest innovations ever achieved occur by the coincidental convergence of multiple adjacent innovations. The upshot is that today, birds can fly and we can see because nature innovated the adjacent possible.

The idea of the adjacent possible applies in the same way to the realm of human ideas. As described in Steven Johnson's *Where Good Ideas Come From*, the best innovations of civilization follow a similar pattern of exploration of adjacent possibilities.[2] From the vacuum tube to GPS to the World Wide Web, Johnson demonstrates that these most important ideas grew by expanding step by step through a series of adjacent ideas, some of which are at first conflicting, or at least confusing. This is powerfully demonstrated today in the iPad, a product hailed as magical and revolutionary by its creator, but which in fact was dependent on all the adjacencies explored by many companies before it. In fact, the history of touch-tablet devices shows that the iPad was the descendent of a long line of innovative precursors, including the GRiDPad from 1989, AT&T's EO PC from 1993, and the PalmPilot family, first launched in 1996—all adjacent possibilities to the computing devices that came before.[3]

That's not a criticism, it's an acknowledgment of the power of innovating the adjacent possible. The most powerful ideas consciously draw from and incorporate elements that were being developed by others along the way, ultimately generating the best outcome in the shortest time at the most efficient cost. This is exactly how Jawbone arrived at the Jambox, adhering to three specific principles of innovating the adjacent possible that we must learn in order to do it successfully.

1. Seek the adjacent possible.
2. Depend on convergent adjacencies.
3. Persist in the path of innovation.

1. Seek the Adjacent Possible

Start with the adjacent possible, *not* the ideal possible. Starting back with the company's Bluetooth headsets, Jawbone was first successful because it asked a simple question, over and over again: What is the next thing my customer needs? Travis had plenty of examples of innovation to offer which might daunt and impress an outsider. These ideas were not particularly revolutionary; ensuring a comfortable fit for the headset may seem like a fancy feature, but it's really the logical next step after you've built a working device. It's an adjacent customer concern. The same is true for more environmentally friendly packaging that is also see-through. Both things will provide adjacent benefits to consumers, yet they are at odds with one another. Because Jawbone iterates so quickly from one adjacency to the next, the team there was able to rapidly identify those desired benefits and to serve both of them simultaneously. An obsession with design helps, but it was really just the commitment to give the customer the next logical thing—or things, in this case—that led Jawbone to desire, design, and deliver a better product experience.

The real trick for Jawbone, however, was seeing that at the end of the Jawbone headset product path was yet another adjacent possibility: a Bluetooth mobile speaker. In many ways, this jump to Jambox seems counterintuitive and even questionable. But because the company was focused on its customers' *mobile* lifestyles, it was able to see that the next thing those people could use was even more mobile audio benefits, such as speakerphone capability and easy access to room-filling music on the go. By focusing on its customers' adjacent possibilities, Jawbone not only made decisions others could not justify, it successfully took over the market with the resulting product.

2. Depend on Convergent Adjacencies

Because it depended on convergent agencies, the original Jawbone headset could not have been invented from scratch by any single company. Instead, it was assembled from the converging technologies surrounding the headset business: Bluetooth technology, long-lasting batteries, lightweight metals, even the smartphone itself. These were all critical adjacencies that made Jawbone's efforts possible. The same applies to Jambox, a product that was an adjacent possibility for its customers but wasn't an adjacent possibility for the company until key technologies converged, like improved Bluetooth chipsets, even better batteries, improved Bluetooth connection implementations in phones and tablets, and the arrival of a software app model so that Jambox could become a mini-platform for audio apps. These in turn will allow developers and consumers to explore even more adjacent possibilities on Jambox.

And that's part of the secret. In the first stage of generating more ideas more quickly by innovating the adjacent possible, a company like Jawbone will come up with many more ideas than they can actually carry out. If the people in the product team are doing their job in truly understanding the customer, they should generate many ideas that aren't even feasible yet. That's a good thing. But how do you whittle that list down? Simply turn to your own adjacent possibilities—consider the converging adjacencies inside or outside your company that make it possible for you to develop and deliver your product. You will then be able to identify the intersection between your customer's adjacent possibilities and your own. In that intersection of converging adjacencies lies the thing your customer most wants which you are most rapidly able to deliver.

Jawbone did exactly that in identifying that people needed more mobile-lifestyle benefits, such as speakerphone capability and access to portable music. The company then identified that it had all the converging abilities it needed—the expertise to pull together improvements in Bluetooth technology, advances in materials science, and the evolution of the consumer software model—to deliver such a device, and Jambox was born. Seen in this light, it's not a market-challenging next product for Jawbone, but an obvious one.

3. Persist in the Path of Innovation

It was just a year after Jambox was introduced that Jawbone released Big Jambox, a $299 bigger brother to the original device. The new speaker is bigger and louder, designed to provide benefits that reach beyond—and are adjacent to—the original. Though less portable, the additional power of the device and the strength of its batteries means it can provide benefits under a wider range of circumstances, whether while cooking in a noisy kitchen or partying hard at the beach.

Innovating the adjacent possible leads you to the next thing your customer needs, even if that thing is not exactly the product you originally designed. Jawbone saw a need for more power and so it delivered that power. But because the company is continually looking for new adjacencies, it wasn't just the size of the device that the product team improved. At the same time, both the original Jambox and Big Jambox were upgraded to provide 3D sound through the company's LiveAudio technology.

Using this framework, a company like Jawbone will eventually land on the ideal innovation we started the chapter imagining. It's not about imagining an ideal end state. The wisdom comes from innovating rapidly from adjacent possibility to adjacent possibility. In this model, we do not predict the future of our product. We start with the next possible thing our customer needs and let the future find us.

———

Now I'll answer the question I asked at the beginning of this chapter: How can our team—composed of mere humans—generate one hundred times more idea power than we generated last year? You know that you can't use either of the traditional approaches that have historically focused on ideal or incremental innovation. Instead, you have to summon and then master the power of innovating the adjacent possible, the way Jawbone did. But how?

Here's how to get started. Picture your customer at the center of a circle defined by their experience of your product or service. Imagine that that customer has certain fundamental needs (as we described in the last chapter) that your current product experience will no longer satisfy.

If you do not change your product experience, that is, if you do not expand it to encompass more of your customer's needs, that customer will step outside of your circle and be subject to temptation from the siren call of a competitor who is meeting those needs. For as long as there has been management science, companies have tried to keep their customers within those circles, tying them down, increasing switching costs, inhibiting their search for more fulfillment, distracting them from any attractive alternatives that came along. What we learned when the internet emerged, however, was that people could switch with very little effort.[4]

This is why innovating the adjacent possible is so necessary. And that is why looking at your customer standing inside your product experience can be so instructive. You owe it to yourself to imagine what need-quenching benefits might tempt them to step out of your circle and evolve in the direction of a competitive offering. What thing could lure them to step away? Ignore competitors. Instead, focus on your customer's psychology, the way the people at Jawbone did when they invented the Jambox. Ask: What does my customer need next?

To do this, you must accept that your customer can leave you without any compunction or hesitation. This is anathema to traditional marketers, I know, but after breathing into a paper bag for a while, you'll be okay. In fact, you'll be happier, because you'll have accepted a crucial truth about your customer. Then ask yourself: Given my customer's relative freedom to fulfill his or her needs, what thing does my customer genuinely need next? What nearby or adjacent possibilities for fulfillment exist?

In our workshops, once we get people started in the right direction—and as long as senior executives present in the room do not object to honesty—people typically list dozens of things that their customers want that they are not currently getting from their existing product experience. Just as Jawbone's team had permission to think of things that annoy customers—like getting makeup on the headset—as opportunities to solve rather than problems to bury, most product teams I work with similarly know ways the product could be improved, ranging from the fundamental to the peripheral.

This is the point at which the excuses start to slip in. "Well, of course, we would like to provide this specific adjacent benefit to our customers, but we can't because of X or Y." Making excuses is as human as breathing. In 1998, when I sat with a large retailer or automaker and they gave me excuse after excuse about why they couldn't do the right thing for their customers, their strategy made sense. Why? Because no one else in their competitive set was able to justify making a disruptive investment, resulting in a stalemate that would perpetuate the status quo.

We no longer live in 1998, especially when we consider the range of competitors who are looking at the same adjacent benefit that we have just identified as one our consumers would respond to if given the chance. Too often, these competitors are coming at that same adjacent possibility from a completely different place—one that has digitally disruptive economics.

Take Netflix. It has been the darling of online media services since 2007, when the company announced it would launch its streaming service. Now, at over 27 million subscribers, Netflix can claim it was a powerful disruptor, that it provided adjacent benefits that created so much value that both Amazon and Comcast are imitating it.

But Netflix has since fallen into trouble, having effectively painted itself into a corner. By focusing narrowly in recent years on incremental improvements in its streaming service, the company has failed to understand that a competitive threat from Amazon is game-changing—because Amazon doesn't have to make money from streaming video. It views streaming video as a customer retention play. And a very adjacent one, at that, because Amazon already has a digital relationship with its customers, and when looking around to see what adjacent benefits it could offer those existing customers, Amazon saw that a video streaming service, even one that didn't generate revenue, would provide hours of enjoyment for them.

That's why another company's adjacent possibility may actually seem like an adjacent *impossibility* to you, one that you would really like to ignore. But to a nontraditional competitor—typically a digital disruptor operating on the assumption of different economics—the adjacent possibility in question is obvious and easy.

At this point, once I have navigated around or over any excuses people want to make for why they can't pursue adjacent possibilities of interest to their customers, I tell them that the instinct to make excuses is actually a healthy one, if we use it properly.

Because we can easily identify a dozen or even several dozen adjacent possibilities that our imaginary customer has before him or her, we have to prioritize those possibilities before we pursue them, and the same cynical part of the mind that makes excuses can fire away at the myriad of options we have identified. Here's the formula:

Evaluate 1) the desirability of the benefit, 2) how proximal the benefit is to the consumer, 3) how easily the company can deliver that benefit with existing resources, and 4) how convenient or elegant the company can make the delivery of the benefit.

The first two items on the list are consumer-centric. How much does the consumer want the benefit, and how easy is it for that consumer to reach out and get that benefit? Items three and four involve turning inward to determine whether or not the company can actually give the customer what they want. This is where the blue-sky C-level executives imagining ideal innovation go wrong—their ideas founder on the challenge of what the company is capable of.

This process works quickly; working with clients, we can usually get a group of smart people halfway there in a four-hour workshop. The reason for this is simple. Most people in big organizations are smarter about their customers than they realize. They just need permission to think about their customers' needs first and they need encouragement to imagine that the company's purpose is to deliver customer benefits quickly and easily rather than to perpetuate existing market structures and models.

Companies have not had the motivation to think like this before. Now they do, because they know that some digital disruptor out there is thinking like this, ready to swoop down and provide adjacent benefits that people really value.

Let's review what we've done here. Have we really learned how to innovate more powerfully?

1. Seek the adjacent possible. Brainstorm all the benefits our customer (or intended customer) might want next. Seek adjacent possibilities, not just incremental or even ideal possibilities.

2. Depend on convergent adjacencies. If you have truly identified your customers' needs instead of your own corporate aspirations, then you will naturally encounter many convergent adjacencies. You can depend on them to shape your adjacent possibility or benefit into a product offering. These can be innovations you will rely on, such as voice recognition technology, Google maps APIs, ad networks, low-cost server technology, or cheap cameras. Make these convergent adjacencies explicit in your planning because they will largely determine the speed and accuracy of your eventual delivery.

3. Persist in the path of innovation. Identifying a list of adjacent possibilities and prioritizing the top three or four that fit your business is not enough. You still have to figure out whether those adjacent possibilities are adjacencies for your business. That will require a vision of what those adjacent possibilities look like when packaged as products or services. Then you have to determine whether you have the skills and resources necessary to get the job done. Finally you must decide what kind of business outcome—including financial return—you expect from it if you do it well.

We'll show you how to do this in the chapters that follow.

7

Deliver Total Product Experiences

What your company sells is no longer just a product (or service). The product is now at the center of a total product experience. Unless you realize this, you'll get outmaneuvered by digital disruptors whose products may not be as good, but who offer better experiences.

As my colleagues Harley Manning and Kerry Bodine describe in their book *Outside In: The Power of Putting Customers at the Center of Your Business*, the experience your customers have is the most powerful force determining the future of your business. But that experience extends far beyond the simple product to everything associated with it—the total product experience.[1]

What is a total product experience? Total product experiences wrap around and through a product, even a very analog product, to amplify, expand, and digitally redefine the way a consumer experiences a product. Total product experiences include analog elements—like what it feels like to open the box or call customer service—and digital elements—your website, your Facebook page, your app, and everything else that extends your product into the digital environment. Because this digital component can improve the product experience so much with so little effort, it radically redefines how your customers perceive, use, and derive satisfaction from your core product. Plus, it creates a two-way channel that also gives you access to real-time information about those customers.

While that sounds (and is) wonderful, note that at the same time, total product experiences wipe out all prior guard rails that protected a product from outside meddling. The converging adjacencies we learned about in the last chapter—the same ones that enable the rapid expansion of your product experience—lead dozens of other companies to the same expanded product definition that you have envisioned. This intensifies competition.

———

Let's imagine you sell an analog product, say, casual shoes for office or after-hours wear. Like any shoes, these are designed, manufactured, ordered, shipped, and put out on display. Perhaps they catch the eye of a shopper, perhaps a store associate looking to bump up the department's sales figures recommends a pair. The shopper who tries them on either buys them or doesn't. The product experience of the shoes pretty much begins and ends there, to be resurrected each time the buyer looks at the shoes sitting in his or her closet and considers whether to don them anew. Beginning and end of product experience.

But shoes aren't just shoes any more—no article of clothing is, as FaceCake Marketing Technologies reveals. FaceCake's CEO Linda Smith aims to extend the product experience of every piece of clothing in the world. In her demo, Linda stands in a plain black dress in front of a large mirror. Reflecting back is her image, although it's slightly altered because what we're seeing isn't really a mirror, it's a large-screen TV enhanced with a Kinect camera, the same 3D-sensing camera for the Xbox 360 that is now in over twenty-two million homes around the world.

Alongside her image in this "mirror" is a menu of clothing and accessories that Linda can, by extending her hand to one side, virtually grab and then place on her body. Check out any one of the various videos featuring the company on YouTube and you can watch Linda or other members of her team as they effortlessly try on dozens of dresses, coats, belts, purses, necklaces, and even shoes.[2]

Using off-the-shelf hardware running sophisticated algorithms, this simple-seeming mirror allows an individual not only to visualize themselves in a new item of clothing, but to move freely with the item on, seeing how it flows as the wearer pivots as well as how it matches with accessory after accessory. This might sound like science fiction, except that FaceCake has partnered with Microsoft to put this technology in Bloomingdale's stores; I also expect this experience to find its way into millions of Xbox 360–powered homes soon.

With technology provided by FaceCake and its competitors, that humble pair of casual shoes (and every other piece of clothing) has a new, digitally enhanced product life. It is part of a total product experience that begins in the moment that the digital mirror provided by FaceCake recommends shoes to perfectly accessorize the new look you just virtually slipped into. You can try the shoes before they have even been put out on the display racks at the store. You'll even be able to sample the shoes before they have been manufactured.

The suggestive sell, however, is just the beginning. Imagine that the same interface is lurking in your closet, where a digital mirror doubles as a fashion consultant that has a complete database of all of your clothing. This virtual consultant could recommend outfits based on what's on your agenda for the day, what the weather forecast looks like, what fashion bloggers you follow, and what you have historically worn on days like today. It could even notice that you've lost a few pounds and offer outfit combinations that would highlight your new more slender physique.

Suddenly, the shoes offer an amplified product experience, one that is intertwined with every other product in the closet as well as every product the personal digital shopping assistant recommends that you add to your collection.

In case you think this is a bit out there, recognize that increasing numbers of consumers now interact daily with digital devices from computers to smartphones to tablets. The customer experience delivered by any company from a bank to an airline to a restaurant to, yes, a clothing manufacturer, is moderated through these devices and their GPS location detection, their Bluetooth connections, their cameras, and crucially, their constant internet connections. Because of these devices, every object you own is now surrounded with a cloud of information, services, and relationship-enhancing value.

That's total product experience and it changes everything.

Designers, manufacturers, fashion magazines, retailers—these are all companies that once had clear boundaries around them. They knew what their job was. Once total product experiences take over, that confidence will evaporate. Because who has a right to own the customer experience of accessorizing a new dress? Is it the dress maker? The accessory maker? The magazine that's promoting the dress? The store that's selling the dress? What about the maker of the digital mirror in her closet? Everyone who touches the experience of that dress now wants to own that customer. That's why Linda, after nearly a decade of hard work building the FaceCake technology, is suddenly in the intersection between all these companies as they realize that with digital disruption, their products are not just products any more, but experiences.

Digital disruptors think in total product experiences. This is a way to conceive of products that forces everyone involved in a product or service, whether manufacturer, marketer, or distributor, to reevaluate their role. Thinking this way rapidly leads them to the conclusion that they ought to make a play for more control over the way the product is experienced by the customer; that is, before someone else in the channel realizes that the same opportunity calls out to them.

———

A week before writing this chapter, I met up with an IT executive of a European airline in Paris. I had just come off the stage where I had presented the idea of total product experience to a room full of IT executives from a variety of industries. After the speech, this executive bounded up to me, his excitement palpable. "This is exactly what I have been trying to tell my company," he said. "We are no longer just selling seats on a plane. We are selling a total travel experience that is wrapped in a digital envelope."

I found it encouraging to hear his description of one of the world's most analog experiences—sitting in a plane, physically rushing through the air at thirty thousand feet—as being primarily a digital experience. It showed that he understood the change that's happening to even the most analog of industries. His most pressing point, however, was not just that change was happening, but that any company that failed to participate in this shift would be pushed right out of the customer's consideration set. Because, as he pointed out, why would a customer choose a product that is not amplified by a digital experience, when digital is available?

Maybe you're a fan of retro experiences and you want to protest by offering up the fact that just last month you bought a vinyl record album to play on your old school turntable at home. No digital product experience there, right? But where did you find out about that album? That artist? Did you check in to the LP store on Foursquare? Did you post a review of your new purchase on Facebook?

If you did, you constructed a very digital total product experience around your very hipster, analog purchase. For the past several years, people have described what you did on Facebook, Twitter, or Foursquare as engaging in social media. But social media in service of a product experience is not just media, it's the experience of the product itself. And it's an experience that the people selling those products desperately want to influence as well as learn from.

From a digital disruptor's point of view, the first motivation in these total product experiences is the customer relationship. Rethinking product is a key way that disruptors establish digital customer relationships, two-way relationships that allow them to test and refine all the adjacent possibilities they need to rapidly evaluate as they innovate their products. They rely on iterative feedback from consumers to tell them whether or not the product innovation works.

It's hard for many companies to adapt to this need for a customer relationship. That's why, so often, the companies that succeed are outsiders to the industry, people who don't have a problem taking on a customer relationship. They often lack the legacy privacy policies that prohibit established players from collecting data and using it in new ways.

Take Netflix. It wasn't the only company that wanted to stream digital video to consumers over the internet. But it was the one that had millions of consumers in a database. Knowing their preferences allowed Netflix to rapidly identify and suggest digital videos they could easily watch. Now, many millions of new customers later, Netflix has more video subscribers than anyone except HBO. And it knows them all by name, something HBO can't say, at least not yet.

Charles Teague and his team at FitNow, the makers of the Lose It! app, were not the only people interested in giving consumers a way to track their calorie consumption. But by defining their total product experience in the optimal way, FitNow has more than 10 million customers on file, about whom they know intimate details such as how much they weigh, what they eat, and how hard they're working to get the pounds off.

Seen in this light, it's no surprise that Jawbone, maker of the Jambox I'm listening to right now, invites users to log in to MyTALK, an app-store-like experience that infuses a digital customer relationship into my already digital speaker. MyTALK does the basics, like upgrading the software on the box as improvements are made available, but it also allows me to swap out the voices the box uses to communicate with me, and it offers audio apps that compel me to use the Jambox for more purposes each day, from speakerphone to remote music box.

All of these measurable experiences from all of these providers report back to the company, practically in real time, making it clear very rapidly how users are responding to a new video player, a new weight loss tracking tool, or a new audio app.

Reviewing this, I propose that digital disruptors embrace a new metric for consumer engagement: minutes per day.[3]

Netflix knows how many minutes you spend in its menus each day and how many minutes you spend watching video. FitNow knows how many minutes you spend logging food and logging your weight. It knows how much time you spend interacting with other Lose It! users. And Jambox can get reports from its devices of how many minutes they are in use, and for which purposes.

Minutes per day, per customer. That's the metric that everyone should be watching. That's the metric that digital disruptors keep their eye on. And it's the metric that a total product experience, when done right, can cause to swell to unheard-of proportions. And if you don't do the same, you'll find that all the customer loyalty you measured in quarterly brand tracking studies has disappeared, replaced by the many minutes your customer now spends with other total product experience providers.

In the past, how much time did you spend thinking about that pair of casual office shoes? Maybe a few minutes a month. Even while you have them on, you probably don't think about them much. But how often will you be able to think about those shoes when they are paired with other virtual items in your shopping cart or your personal closet? And how much would a company that makes shoes like to know which shoes got more minutes of your attention?

———

Thinking in product experiences is going to take some training. I know because my colleagues and I have been teaching it to people for more than two years. You may think that what I'm telling you is obvious, because it is—just like digital disruption is obvious. But time and time again, as we share this product innovation process with real people in real companies, once people get past the need to act like they already know how to do this and once they admit that their company isn't leading the world in product innovation, then they start to discuss the real barriers to building total product experiences. That's the whole purpose of this exercise. We call it CBSP, which stands for the four elements you need to evaluate: customer, benefits, strategy, and product. Most importantly, you must *start* with customers.[4]

Customers

Start by understanding the customer you want to reach with the product experience you will eventually create. When you start with the customer, even before you have conceived your product experience innovation, you can be completely honest with yourself about who those people really are.

Here's an example. I conducted a workshop with a large media company that was developing a new media product. When I asked who their target customer for this media product would be, they responded, proudly, that they had a complete profile of the five million women they were developing this experience for. Five million? That kind of number is the first place I can spot a post-hoc rationalized customer. Because nobody has had the guts to pinpoint the actual personalities, drives, urges, and needs of a real target customer, they instead rely on large, demographically defined customer groups. But this kind of thinking fails to get at the needs that, as we described in chapter 5, are the fundamental drivers of product adoption.

A bit of investigation with this client revealed that they needed to sell fifty thousand products to be successful. So I asked, "Can you tell me what you think those fifty thousand people want that will make them buy this product?" Happily, they started to spill over with ideas—assumptions about the likely buyer that were enlightening and even inspiring. They seemed to have such a great sense of who this customer was that I was forced to ask them why they had withheld all of this richness earlier, when I had asked who the target was.

The answer was plain. They needed to give upper management a large number to start with in order to get the green light on developing the product experience. But by not insisting on a more targeted number, upper management was not requiring the team to clearly identify the motivations of the customers they eventually hoped to captivate.

Motivations are crucial, far more crucial than massive numbers of potential "customers," most of whom don't actually want the product. So I hereby give you permission to think big by thinking small, by isolating the core target customers and making some really smart guesses about what makes them tick.

As a traditional researcher who has conducted more focus groups and led more surveys than I dare count, I am in a unique position to tell you that you *don't* have to start with slow, expensive traditional research techniques to innovate your product experience. So start making the smartest guesses you can about what makes your customer likely to respond to your innovative product. Use your knowledge of the marketplace to get yourself moving. Start with your current product experience and then expand your view to your most successful competitors. Why do the leading products succeed? Don't fall for pat explanations that are summed up in a single word or phrase like "brand" or "customer experience." Of course those are important, but those are attributes of the product, not the customer!

Instead, explain successes from the perspective of the customer. Using the framework in chapter 5, ask yourself what your target customer really needs. Describe those needs in conversational phrases like, "people need to feel that they are part of a trend that is bigger than themselves," which could apply to such diverse product experiences as best-selling books, new mascara, or electric cars. Note that this statement maps to two human needs: *connection* because customers are connecting to other people through the trend, and *uniqueness* because the trend customers align with helps them feel that they are part of the *right* group of people.

Once you are living in these people's shoes, once you are standing within their needs and opportunities, you are then perfectly poised to take the next step in CBSP: benefits.

Benefits

Resist the temptation to skip ahead to product ideas. Now you know what these people need at a fundamental level, but you haven't expressed their needs in concrete benefits that you can offer them. The best way to do this is to innovate some adjacent possibilities. Thus equipped with a sense of the customer (even if it's just a guess at this point), you are in a position to ask yourself, "What is the *next* thing that customer needs?"

But don't try to invent the product at this point. Express the need in terms of what the customer will get out of the deal if you succeed. "People will get a way to be visibly committed to the environment," for electric cars. "Our customers will know that they have a new applicator for mascara that is superior to the applicator other people use," for cosmetics. "People will experience the heartwarming sensation of knowing that they're reading a powerful book that a million other people are also reading right now," for a bestseller.

To get started, focus on one C (customer) and offer only a handful of Bs (benefits) to those customers. If you try to multiply your offering before you have even innovated it, you will revert to the lowest common denominator product and impair your capacity for innovation. This is because no product experience is all the things its designers claim it is. Remember, R&D teams have a tendency to confuse product features with customer benefits. They assume that more features equals more benefits. This is not true. Especially when the overcrowding of benefits reduces the product experience or marketing to mush. Look at any spec sheet for a Blu-ray player in Best Buy and you'll see what I mean. Your eyes tend to glaze over after the first one or two in the list of features.

If you have disciplined yourself to focus on one C—at least for now— then you will understand that of the list of forty "benefits" you think you can offer them, there are two or three that really move the needle for the customer you have just gotten very familiar with. Those are the benefits you should keep foremost in mind as you move through the remaining steps in the process.

Go through this exercise of connecting C and B as many times as you need to in order to get it and make it second nature. When you do, you will find that the relationship between C (customers) and B (benefits) is comfortably expressed as, "Who do we want to innovate for and what will they get out of it?"

Strategy

While the first half of CBSP is focused on the customer, the second half turns these key questions right around, with the company in mind, to ask, "What will we get out of it if we innovate?" That bit, the "what do we get out of it," is an obvious question but it's also very hard to answer without resorting to overly simple statements like "sell products" or "make money." Stated that way, those are the generic goals of the company, not the innovation process. You need to focus in this stage on the strategic outcome that you want to get if you give that C the B that you have just identified.

This is where not only can you be selfish and company-focused, but you must. It doesn't betray the customer for the company to be successful, after all. Make the S in CBSP one of the most straightforward steps in the model.

Identify a measurable success the company will gain, such as:

- We want to sign up 5,000 customers in the first week
- We want to extend minutes of engagement by 5 minutes per user per day
- We want to collect 20 percent more data per customer than we currently have on existing customers.

It is okay to say you want to sell more product or make more money. You just have to own up to it by putting a hard metric on the sales you want or the revenue you expect so that you can tie the incremental outcome for the company to your specific innovation. If you can't measure it, you can't say whether you succeeded, and chances are, it's not digitally disruptive.

Product

If you have done C, B, and S right, P has been nagging at you all along. Ideas have been suggesting themselves, some of them obvious and some of them more surprising. If you have disciplined yourself, you have resisted the urge to talk product before now.

Now you can go for it. Let's consider an example, a team that is trying to determine how they can take an old line of casual shoes that were once popular and pivot the shoe's appeal to reach a new and potentially younger audience.

For the customer in this case, the target C is someone interested in a new type of shoe, someone who may think that the old brand hasn't kept up with the times. The team has dug deep into an analysis of successful competitors who are capturing this customer and have hypothesized that this customer base feels energized by variety, by new things that are shiny and intriguing, and therefore might be a bit embarrassed to turn to this old brand. The team wants to offer these customers a B that involves repositioning the brand to be self-consciously ironic and retro, to make the old deliberately new and therefore juxtapose the traditional brand message with a new product experience that is undeniably innovative. The S, or strategic outcome, the company wants is to have a digital customer relationship with fifty thousand of these new customers.

Now that we're at P, we can finally ask what this product innovation might look like. The list here can and should be long as you try to identify the exact experience that will convey the short list of benefits promised. You could update the materials the product is made of to make it seem just a bit newer or to play up its retro hipness. You could embed a technology sensor into the shoe that reports on the steps owners take with the shoe. You could create a Facebook page that encourages people to post photos of their new shoes in ironic, retro contexts. Though the list could easily be longer, let's consider these three ideas given the customers, the benefits we want to offer them, and the strategic outcome we want for the company.

Modifying the materials the shoe is made of may stimulate new interest in the target customers. If done right, it could certainly offer them the benefit we believe they want. But would it create the opportunity to create a digital relationship with fifty thousand shoe buyers? Not by itself.

Embedding a wireless pedometer into the shoe can certainly lead to the strategic outcome we want because it would create a measurable digital bridge between the customer and the company, just as digital disruptors always do. But does this alone create the benefit we believe these people want? That would depend on what kind of total product experience we build on top of that digital bridge.

Finally, a Facebook page, if designed with the right customer in mind, might stimulate people's interest in a new shoe. And if we ask people to "like" the page or install the app, it certainly gives the company a digital relationship with the customers who chose to interact with the app. But does it appeal to the C that we so desperately want to reach?

You can see that the value of being explicit about CBSP is that it forces you to be honest about your intentions and your hopes. It also pinpoints when you have skipped ahead to P without rigorously defining C and B, as is very likely the case with the Facebook page. You can see how that could happen: Someone on the team would have imagined a really cool app based on something they saw Starbucks do, but did not follow the discipline of asking, "For whom would that be cool and what benefit would they derive from it?"

Note that each of these three innovations is imperfect at least on some level. This is always the case, and it provides the decision makers in the team or division with the explicit statement of the hopes and ambitions of the product innovation so that they can iteratively reevaluate whether they are following the CBSP model optimally.

It is also likely that you could tie all three of these things together: Make the outside of the shoe look different enough to suggest to our new customer that things are changing, then add a sensor to the shoe that encourages a digital relationship with the customer, and create a page on Facebook that forwards what you learn from the shoe to your friends in a potentially competitive way to stimulate interest. From this solution, you see that the product experience is expanding dramatically, but in ways that are targeted very clearly to the customer the company wants to reach.

You get the sense from this example that the art of P is the art of harmonizing C, B, S, and P into a single approach. That harmonization requires iteratively applying CBSP until you create the innovations that are most likely to give the consumers you want to reach the benefits they really desire while achieving strategic outcomes that are meaningful to the organization. Then you rinse and repeat. In this case, I would encourage this team not to overlook its current buyer. What possible effect might these enhancements to the product have on them? Can we take up the company's traditional C and describe the appropriate B in a way that could allow us to kill two Ss with one P?

That's CBSP in a nutshell. If you use it often, it becomes a mental checklist to help you verify that you're not suggesting innovation for innovation's sake, but that you're innovating in the interests of your customer while explicitly tying those interests to the interests of the company. The result of a CBSP exercise typically shows the team just how far outside of their traditional product boundaries they could consider stepping.

———

Think this doesn't apply to you? Well, I once sat across the table from a consumer insights expert at one of the largest consumer packaged goods manufacturers in the world. She had recently heard me give a speech about total product experiences and her first reaction was that she was unimpressed.

"Sure, that's true for technology and other innovative products, but I'm selling feminine hygiene, shampoo, and toothpaste," she explained. "These are not digital products."

Then she went home and checked it herself. She jumped onto the Apple App Store and started searching for the same keywords that she routinely used in marketing campaigns and search engine optimization exercises for her products. What she saw practically made her jaw drop.

As she later told me, "There were hundreds of apps designed to help women track their monthly cycles, develop regimens for skin care, or track their pregnancies. And that's when I realized that these total digital product experiences were already happening, using technology my customers already have in their hands, and effectively removing my influence from the products and services that those total product experiences were promoting."

I couldn't have said it better myself.

If you're feeling a sense of urgency, good. But you may also be feeling a sense of impending doom. If you're like most people in most companies, you are not sure your company can do all of this. You're not sure your company can adopt the digital disruptor's mindset or behave like a digital disruptor. You realize that you must first unleash the digital disruptor inside your organization before you can let that digitally disruptive energy out on the marketplace. It's time to disrupt yourself now.

PART 4

Disrupt Yourself Now

8

Assess Your Digital Disruption Readiness

Any company of any size can become a digital disruptor. The employees must adopt a digital disruptor's mindset and behave like digital disruptors. Obviously, this is not easy. Each company has its own challenges and obstacles it must overcome in order to shift from prior ways of doing business. The larger the company, the harder the task it is. And the further you are from sources of power in the company, the less optimistic you may be about this change. But whatever challenges your company faces, none of them are impossible to overcome. In this chapter I offer you hope—a digitally disruptive example from one of the largest companies on the globe—and a tool for assessing exactly which demons your company has to wrestle with compared to others around the world.

For the most part, Tim FitzRandolph is just like other mobile game developers. He beavers away on mobile-game ideas in his spare time to improve his skills and think through interesting ideas. He posts mobile games that are less than awesome just to get some feedback and see how people respond. But what makes Tim different is this: He works at Disney, and he got to be disruptive right in the middle of a large, well-established company.

Disney has repeatedly claimed it would one day take its rightful place in the internet entertainment universe. It has the brand strength and the money to pursue a significant share of the attention of interactive device users of all ages. But it's never managed to achieve breakout success with mobile gaming, even as games like Angry Birds and Cut the Rope rose up to swallow hours of consumer media time. At least, that was the case until Tim and his team created a mobile app called Where's My Water?, the only mobile game created by a major media company to reach the top slot in the mobile game world, both in Apple's App Store and Google Play. In a market where its direct competitor, Viacom, with its hot SpongeBob property, develops apps that barely score tens of thousands of downloads, Disney's Where's My Water? has achieved tens of millions.

How did Tim and Disney do it? Could your company do this? Tim's story begins to tell us how.

Tim worked his way up the corporate ladder, starting in quality assurance for several of Disney's gaming efforts. He was promoted to producer for a game based on a sequel of a traditional Disney property. Moving his family around as he was transferred from one division to another, Tim spent some time on console games, eventually landing in the mobile games team.

In all this time, Tim did not see himself as a digital disruptor to the industry that he served. But he certainly acted like one. Eager to sharpen his skills, he spent his free time developing games of all sorts. He eventually created a little game called Jelly Car which he released as freeware on the IndieGames community on Xbox Live in early 2008, later updating it for the iPhone when the App Store was created.

He did this while working full-time at Disney Interactive Studios, a game development team inside the massive Disney enterprise. In a typical media business, the powers that be would treat the release of an independent game from an employee as a direct assault on its core business. But because Tim thinks and acts like a digital disruptor, he didn't even imagine that Disney would have a problem with his efforts. As he explains, "I did not ask the official permission to do these games on the side, I just did it. I was never challenged on it. I thought, 'If anyone tells me I shouldn't make them anymore, I would just stop.' It never came to that." Instead, the opposite occurred. Tim proposed an adaptation of his game for Disney. The company took a look and liked it. "Some documents had to be signed," he offers modestly. And the official version of Jelly Car was born. It wasn't a smash hit, and even though it's still available today on the iPhone, it was never ported to the Android environment.

Did that make it a failure? No. Because the real value of Jelly Car to Disney was that through it the company learned a few things: 1) Disney had development talent inside the company that it could use to do original projects, and 2) Disney could experiment by developing games that don't involve Disney's traditional characters. It could easily mess around with a game as long as it didn't have the Little Mermaid or Mater or Buzz Lightyear in it.

That drove the discussion forward at Disney. As Tim says, "Seems like this method is a cheaper way to test ideas and innovations. It's certainly much cheaper than a big tentpole movie. We can have more leeway to test things, as long as we're not out of bounds, we can have more autonomy, a little less scrutiny. If this game had failed, it's not like there would be disastrous consequences. We would just learn a lot and try again."

Not long after that, Where's My Water? was the number one game on the App Store. "The whole thing took about eight months total, from the very beginning, from 'Hey, let's make a new game,' two months of that—deciding on the game, then deciding the character and world—then it was six months until we released the game."

Speed is critical to digital disruptors both inside and outside of large companies. Tim explains the secret to their speedy success this way: "We were able to move quickly because we're a small team. It's basically the core team that works on this every day. At the time, we were basically five of us, not counting executives and marketing and things like animation and music."

A small team working on its own could go off the rails, but not this one. "Our leadership here was really helpful in giving us the reins to run with the project, to guide us in the right direction. But they also gave us autonomy to work without turning the ship around in the middle of the project. Most of the decisions were made in the right order with frequent check-ins with upper management. We never had a problem with them saying, 'You guys are way off course' or any issue like that. We were able to plow through development rapidly."

All of this was happening inside the relatively small confines of a mobile gaming unit, which isn't even physically located at Disney's Burbank headquarters. Surely this would have to blow up at some point, right? Not in this case.

"The game just kept getting better and better. We started to get a lot of momentum, it was a very slow kind of snowball.... We got a little more scrutiny as people started to say 'Wow, this character might hit.' Instead [of resistance] we got people volunteering, 'Hey, you might want to pick the brains of these people or those people, we'll make them available to you.'" Then, once the game was released and shot to number one on the App Store, Where's My Water? garnered even more internal support. "The phone calls started coming from other divisions, 'Congratulations, we're big fans, we'd love to talk about potential products.'"

Potential products? Don't forget that Disney is a massive merchandising machine. From *High School Musical* lunchboxes to *Cars* toothpaste, all the Disney-branded merchandise acts as a financial booster in support of the major movies and TV shows that Disney usually invests tens or hundreds of millions of dollars to establish. But in this case, a team of five developers created a hot new property that Disney could spin into merchandise, created at little cost and low risk.

It's digital disruption, from inside the four walls of a massive company, one that normally wouldn't have permitted this to happen, yet did. Is your company ready to do the same?

In October 2011, Forrester Research conducted an online survey of some of our clients' employees, asking: Is your company ready to become a digital disruptor? We focused on three elements of readiness: energy, skills, and policies. A company that wants to think and act like a digital disruptor has to have the right kind of energy, staff with the right skills, and policies than enable digital disruptors to succeed. At Disney, Tim and his team brought a personal enthusiasm to the task that helped them overcome obstacles in a short time frame. They had the digital skills they needed to build a different kind of game from the type the company was asking them to build. And the company's policies never changed, but rather encouraged the development of Where's My Water?.

Energy is first because your people have to be excited about making a digital transition, otherwise no amount of top-down exhortation will make it so. But energy alone can't do it if the people who work there don't have the skills needed to excel in a digital age. Those skills can include the skills needed to manage direct customer relationships, extract insight from new sources of customer data, or envision and build the total product experience your customers will respond to.

Experience taught us that those two things—energy and skills—are insufficient. Because the wrong policies and practices will inhibit or prevent whatever energy and skills that are present from unleashing new product experiences.

As you read these survey results, remember that we surveyed our own global clients, companies that are generally more invested in innovation and digital readiness than the average company. A survey of "average" workers would probably find even less readiness for digital disruption.

What did we find? First of all, digital disruption is highly visible across most industries. Nine out of ten respondents agreed or strongly agreed that there was significant opportunity for digital tools or experiences to change their industry. But were their companies ready? Despite a lot of optimism, the data revealed that many companies were not prepared (see Figure 8-1).

While two-thirds agreed with the statement "My company's relationship with its customers will be stronger in five years," only 48 percent thought their companies would be more innovative in that same time frame.

This should cause great concern. How will these companies have a better relationship with customers, how will they develop best-in-class products and services, if they are not more innovative than other firms? Where will that value come from if not by using the latest technology or by significantly altering products and services in light of the dramatic digital changes that I've just spent eight chapters describing?

Figure 8-1: Respondents are optimistic about their companies but not their innovation

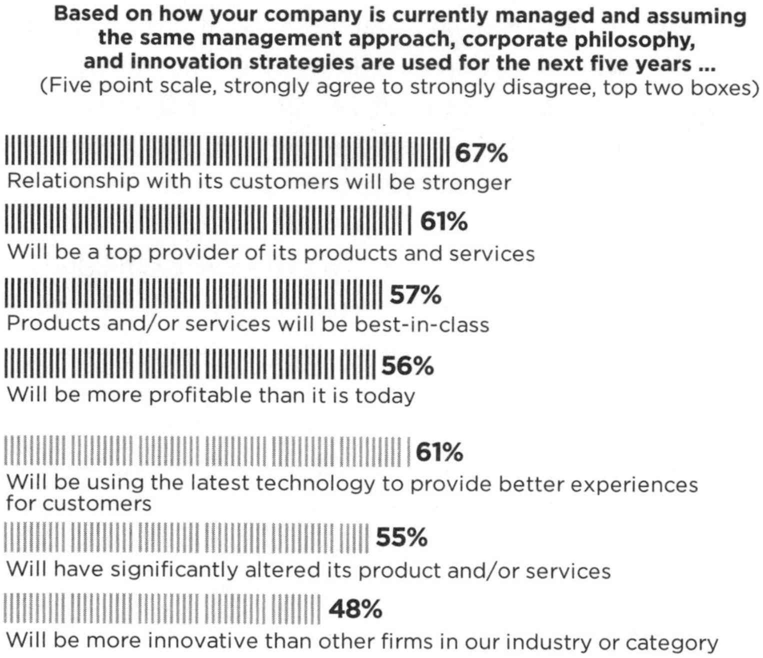

Based on how your company is currently managed and assuming the same management approach, corporate philosophy, and innovation strategies are used for the next five years ...
(Five point scale, strongly agree to strongly disagree, top two boxes)

‖‖‖‖‖‖‖‖‖‖‖‖‖‖‖‖‖‖‖‖‖‖‖‖‖‖‖‖‖‖‖‖‖‖‖‖ **67%**
Relationship with its customers will be stronger

‖‖‖‖‖‖‖‖‖‖‖‖‖‖‖‖‖‖‖‖‖‖‖‖‖‖‖‖‖‖‖‖‖ **61%**
Will be a top provider of its products and services

‖‖‖‖‖‖‖‖‖‖‖‖‖‖‖‖‖‖‖‖‖‖‖‖‖‖‖‖‖‖‖ **57%**
Products and/or services will be best-in-class

‖‖‖‖‖‖‖‖‖‖‖‖‖‖‖‖‖‖‖‖‖‖‖‖‖‖‖‖‖‖ **56%**
Will be more profitable than it is today

‖‖‖‖‖‖‖‖‖‖‖‖‖‖‖‖‖‖‖‖‖‖‖‖‖‖‖‖‖‖‖‖‖ **61%**
Will be using the latest technology to provide better experiences for customers

‖‖‖‖‖‖‖‖‖‖‖‖‖‖‖‖‖‖‖‖‖‖‖‖‖‖‖‖‖ **55%**
Will have significantly altered its product and/or services

‖‖‖‖‖‖‖‖‖‖‖‖‖‖‖‖‖‖‖‖‖‖‖‖‖ **48%**
Will be more innovative than other firms in our industry or category

Base: 285 global executives invited to participate
Source: Forrester Digital Readiness Assessment, June 2012

We find the answer to these questions by looking at the challenges companies face in trying to adapt to digital disruption (see Figure 8-2). Though 87 percent of executives agreed that there is a lot of opportunity for their company to use digital tools to gain competitive advantage, 56 percent of them also believe it is likely companies outside of their industry

Figure 8-2: Employees see digital opportunity, yet expect outsiders to seize it first

How much do you agree the following statements apply to the industry your company is in?
(Five point scale, top two boxes)

||||||||||||||||||||||||||||||||||||||||||||||||||||||||||||||||||||||||||||||||||||| **87%**
How much opportunity is there for your company to use digital tools and experiences to gain competitive advantage in your industry?

|||||||||||||||||||||||||||||||||||||||||||||||||||||||| **56%**
It is very likely that companies outside of our industry will have an easier time using digital tools and experiences to change our industry than for companies currently inside our industry

Base: 285 global executives invited to participate
Source: Forrester Digital Readiness Assessment, June 2012

will have an easier time using digital tools to change their industry. They're not ready.

Let's look at energy, skills, and policies (see Figure 8-3.) Roughly two-thirds of executives agree that people inside the company are excited about digital. It's not an overwhelming majority, but it's a significant share. That's positive, and it's a shift from my reading of my meetings with clients five and even two years ago, when the idea of digital-led change stimulated only fear and, in some cases, loathing.

But only 38 percent of execs think that the people in the company have the skills they need to adapt to digital. That creates an energy-to-skills gap where there's only half as much ability as there is enthusiasm.

Things can get worse, too. When we asked people whether their company has the policies and business practices that will permit them to exploit digital, just 32 percent said yes. Add all of that up—high levels of energy burdened with low levels of skill and poor policies—and it's not surprising that only 37 percent of our respondents expressed confidence that the company would "put the right resources" in place to handle the digital transition.

Figure 8-3: Respondents' companies have the energy, but many lack skills, policies, and resources

How much do you agree the following statements apply to your company?
Level of agreement (five point scale, top two boxes)

||||||||| |||||||| ||||||||| |||||||||| |||||||||| |||||||| ||||| **65%**
People in our company are excited about the changes that digital will bring to our company

||||||||| ||||||||| ||||||||| ||||||| **38%**
People in our company have the skills needed to adapt to the changes that digital will bring to our company

|||||||||| ||||||||| ||||||||| ||| **32%**
Our company has policies and business practices that will enable us to adapt to the changes that digital will bring to our company

||||||||| ||||||||| ||||||||| |||||| **37%**
Our company will put the right resources (people, budget, time) in place to adapt to the changes that digital will bring to our company

Base: 285 global executives invited to participate
Source: Forrester Digital Readiness Assessment, June 2012

There's your benchmark. Is your company excited? So is everyone else's. Does your company have the skills? A majority of executives we surveyed say theirs does not. Do you have the policies and practices needed? Two-thirds say no. Facing your unique combination of energy, skills, and policies, will your company do the right thing? If your company is like these companies, the answer from a majority of employees is no.

It might even be worth an informal survey of your own team. Rather than find out what percent of your team agrees or disagrees with a particular statement, however, I'm going to give you a way to ask them to express the level of intensity of their agreement, and I'll provide you with similar intensity measures from our survey to compare to. Give your team the exercise shown in Table 8-1, or have them do the evaluation online at our website forrester.com/disruption:

Table 8-1. Digital disruption readiness benchmark assessment

Answer the three following questions on a scale from 1 to 10, where 1 = disagree completely and 10 = agree completely	
	People in our company are excited about the changes that digital will bring to our company.
	People in our company have the skills needed to adapt to the changes that digital will bring to our company.
	Our company has policies and business practices that will enable us to adapt to the changes that digital will bring to our company.
	Our company will put the right resources (people, budget, time) in place to adapt to the changes that digital will bring to our company.

Let them answer anonymously, writing a number from 1 to 10 next to each box. You can do this with three people or thirty; either way, just throw their answers in a spreadsheet and average them. Take the four averages and place them in a grid, adding your own individual answers for good measure, as shown in Table 8-2.

Table 8-2: Sample digital disruption readiness benchmark

	Your answers	Team answers (average)	Baseline
Energy	8	7.6	7.1
Skills	7	5.9	5.4
Policies	5	5.3	4.9
Resources	4	5.1	5.4

The first column shows your individual answers on the scale from 1 to 10, the second column are the answers of your team members, averaged, and then I've inserted the baseline scale numbers based on our survey so you can compare yourself and your team to our survey sample.

The first thing to do is to compare the group average to your own individual answer. Are you surprised at how differently your team answered compared to you? What do you think accounts for the differences? Now compare your team's answers to the responses from the other companies. In my example, the team is more optimistic when it comes to energy and skills but less confident when it comes to the policies and resources questions. This comparison is useful as a way to motivate yourself. But it's even more important as a way to help you see what obstacles you face, regardless of what other companies are dealing with.

To get that, let the honest answers sink in. If your team scores your company at 5.3 for policies and practices, congratulations. You are at least slightly ahead of the pack, according to our survey. But if you really think about what that means, you realize that you're still in jeopardy with a 5.3 rating out of 10 because it means that your team is ultimately not confident in your policies and practices. The eye-opening thing about our survey is just how much it educates each of us about how far we have yet to go, regardless of how we stack up against others. Fortunately, it also educates us about what we need to fix. Policies and practices are generally at the top of the to-do list, without which improving skills would be a wasted effort anyway.

This all contrasts, by the way, with people's perception of their own individual abilities and opportunities. To be sure we didn't accidentally survey a bunch of malcontents and misfits, we asked them similar questions about their own situation. Figure 8-4 shows their results. You'll notice that people are more optimistic about their own individual chances.

People are just as likely to be personally excited about the changes digital will bring as they think the rest of the company is. But that's where the similarities between the company and the individuals that work for them end. Nearly three-fourths think they have the skills to adapt to

Figure 8-4: People's answers about themselves show optimism

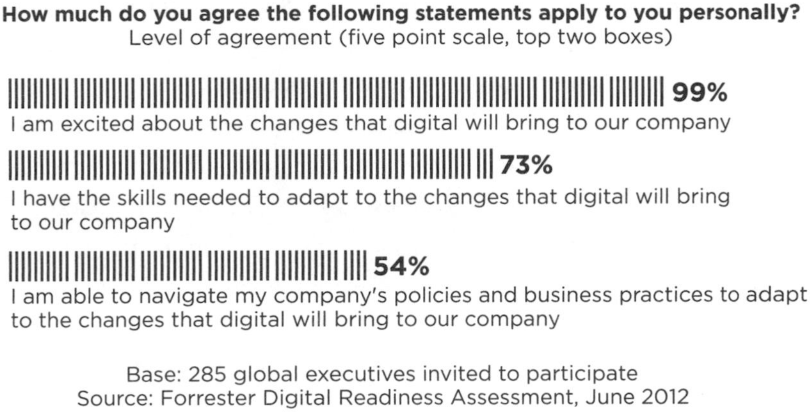

How much do you agree the following statements apply to you personally?
Level of agreement (five point scale, top two boxes)

||||||||||||||||||||||||||||||||||||||||||||||||||||||||||||||||||||||||||||||||||||||||||||||||||||| **99%**
I am excited about the changes that digital will bring to our company

|||||||||||||||||||||||||||||||||||||||||||||||||||||||||||||||||||||||| **73%**
I have the skills needed to adapt to the changes that digital will bring
to our company

|||||||||||||||||||||||||||||||||||||||||||||||||| **54%**
I am able to navigate my company's policies and business practices to adapt
to the changes that digital will bring to our company

Base: 285 global executives invited to participate
Source: Forrester Digital Readiness Assessment, June 2012

digital while a slim majority are confident that they can personally navigate the policies and practices to adapt, even if they thought the company's policies and practices were not the right ones.

Thank heaven for optimists. Without them we'd be lost. Do they really have the skills? Probably not. But even if they have those skills, only half of them think they can navigate the policies and practices of the company.

―――

The central question of this chapter is, "Can you really do this?" I believe you can, despite what I know about the challenges you face. If the energy and the will are there, and at least some portion of the skills are in place, the first thing you need to do to make this work is change the policies and practices that are getting in the way.

One of the biggest structural barriers our clients face is the specialization of silos that have built up over the years. Because companies built up those silos in an era of analog assumptions, each silo took shape under certain expectations about how it would add value to the company. In the face of digital disruption, those silo assumptions become dramatic liabilities that can fatally inhibit a company's response to digital disruption.

Disney could very easily have pushed Tim FitzRandolph and his team down when his efforts popped up in the uncharted regions between silos. Here was a team trying to do things its own way without understanding the flow of value through Disney's historical silos.

Your company likely does the same thing. Because each silo has its own budget, its own impact on the product, and—most detrimental of all—its own metrics for generating bonuses and rewarding team members, more often than not, efforts like Tim's run afoul of the specialization that the company depends on in order to direct the creation and distribution of value.

The bigger the company, the harder it is to overcome these silos. That might help explain why all of our survey responses are significantly more discouraging when we look at the answers through the lens of company size. If we examine companies with more than a thousand employees, we see that the hopeful optimism I praised just a few paragraphs ago is harder to find at large enterprises (see Figure 8-5).

The differences start right from the beginning, with the executives at smaller companies able to generate more enthusiasm for digital than their counterparts in larger companies. The differences get especially challenging at the level of skills, and even more so at policies and practices. The larger the ship, the harder it is to turn in the face of an iceberg.

Does this mean big companies are doomed? Not necessarily. Disney disrupted from within with Where's My Water?, USAA did it when it offered its customers the ability to take a picture of their paycheck to deposit the funds, and HBO did it when it launched HBO GO, as I'll describe in chapter 9. It is possible, even if it is very, very hard.

That's why changes can't begin with nothing more than executive speeches at company meetings that talk optimistically about the future. Those executives must identify and dismantle the policies and practices that will stand in the way. The same executives will have to artfully but energetically breach the silos that have stood independent of one another for so many years. Then, and only then, can they encourage and reward

Figure 8-5: Bigger companies are less optimistic

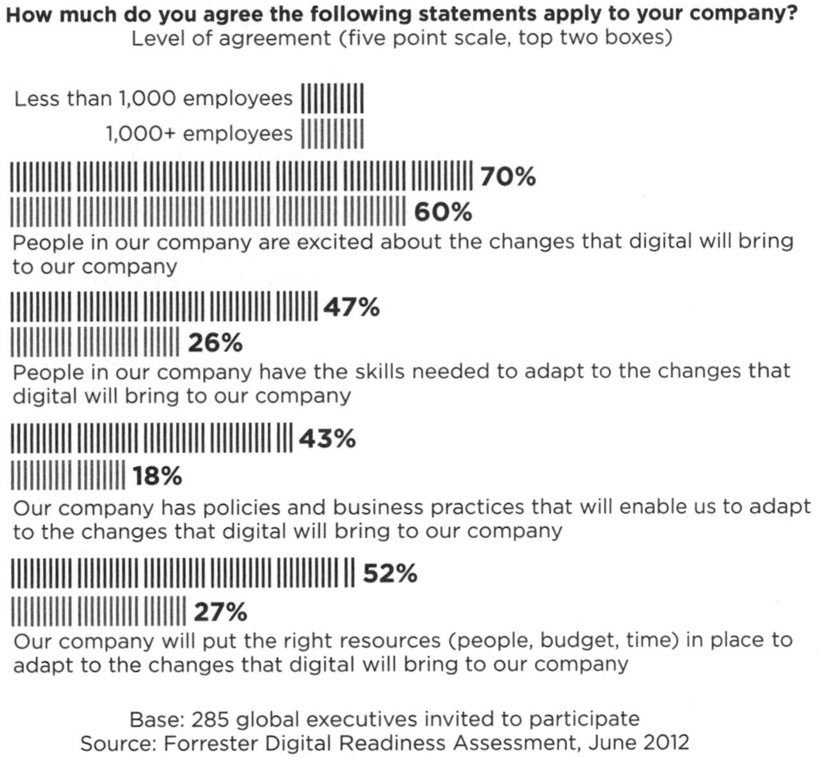

How much do you agree the following statements apply to your company?
Level of agreement (five point scale, top two boxes)

Less than 1,000 employees ||||||||||
1,000+ employees ||||||||||

||||||||| ||||||||| ||||||||| ||||||||| ||||||||| ||||||||| ||||||||| **70%**
||||||||| ||||||||| ||||||||| ||||||||| ||||||||| ||||||||| **60%**
People in our company are excited about the changes that digital will bring
to our company

||||||||| ||||||||| ||||||||| ||||||||| ||||||| **47%**
||||||||| ||||||||| |||||| **26%**
People in our company have the skills needed to adapt to the changes that
digital will bring to our company

||||||||| ||||||||| ||||||||| ||||||||| ||| **43%**
||||||||| |||||||| **18%**
Our company has policies and business practices that will enable us to adapt
to the changes that digital will bring to our company

||||||||| ||||||||| ||||||||| ||||||||| ||||||||| || **52%**
||||||||| ||||||||| ||||||| **27%**
Our company will put the right resources (people, budget, time) in place to
adapt to the changes that digital will bring to our company

Base: 285 global executives invited to participate
Source: Forrester Digital Readiness Assessment, June 2012

the individual enthusiasm resident in the organization from top to bottom, as Disney encouraged Tim's team.

One client we work with—a large maker of consumer products—identified that it was falling behind the traditional competitors within its industry at the same time it faced disruptive innovation from outside its industry. The company made a startling move designed to shake up innovation: It promoted a VP of product development and strategy to chief marketing officer. This sort of disruptive move can cause resentment and anger, but the situation required radical measures. This CMO, in addition to learning the ropes of his new job, quickly assembled an innovation team: four people tasked with generating twelve product ideas, ranging from the immediately obvious to the potentially bizarre, all adjacent to existing customer needs or company capabilities. The CMO then charged the team with creating a prioritization matrix for the ideas in order to identify three that it could develop and test before the end of the year.

I met with a member of this team who showed me prototypes of these three products. This private demo at CES was designed as the final stage of testing for the product ideas. Each one was fully fleshed out and prototypes of either the core technology or the demo finished product were available to deliver an approximate product experience. The team's mission at CES was simple: secure commitments from distributors to buy these product ideas and deliver them to retail channels in that year, or shelve these products and move on to the next three ideas deemed worthy of testing.

The individual who gave me the sneak peek at the product outcomes could barely contain his enthusiasm, not just for the products, but for the process that had generated them. I could practically feel his excitement to be a part of his company's rush into the future. And as I asked him about the process, he was more than happy to identify all the ways that traditional silos had to be breached for this process to work as quickly and effectively as it did.

I wish I could point to retail shelves to show you the outcomes of this process and I hope that someday soon I'll be able to, but this company has already found a couple of points worth emphasizing about how to deal with digital disruption inside a large company:

- Create small innovation teams
- Identify silos and break down the boundaries between them
- Get senior executives to commit their support
- Insist on short development time frames

This list should not come as a surprise because all four of these conditions applied to Tim FitzRandolph's team at Disney. And time and time again, when I see companies take too long, think too much and do too little, or allow infighting to derail cooperation, at least one of these four conditions is missing.

You may have noticed that in the list I didn't say who should do all these wonderful things, I just insisted they have to get done. Obviously, only the most senior executives have the authority to make these kinds of decisions. This is not something a radical innovator or a single team can do, no matter how hard they try. Senior executives have to lead. And therein lies the rub.

In our surveys, there is a dramatic contrast between people who are VPs or above and the other two-thirds that work for them. Senior executives think they're ready to charge boldly forward, but the people who work for them think the company isn't ready (see Figure 8-6).

The differences diverge right from the outset, as lower-downs in the organization chart a less sunny course for the organization, including the stunning drop from 70 percent of executives who think the company will be more innovative than other companies in the same industry compared with 39 percent of lower-level employees.

As people are asked for more detail about their organization's ability to adapt to a digitally disruptive environment, the people lower down the totem pole have a significantly less optimistic outlook. And when it comes to the policies and practices needed to succeed, now we see why the overall enthusiasm is so low: Depending on where you sit in an organization, the policies and practices can seem more daunting. The lower you go, the harder it is to navigate those policies and practices to get the job done.

What should you do? Unless you can promote everyone to VP, perhaps it's time to examine your policies and practices closely. And do it with the help of the people who actually carry out the policy and comply with historical practices. Their input will likely be difficult to hear, but it will be crucial to accommodate.

Figure 8-6: Senior executives believe; the rest of the company, not so much

How much do you agree the following statements apply to your company?
Level of agreement (five point scale, top two boxes)

VP and above ||||||||||
Below VP ||||||||||

|||||||||| |||||||||| |||||||||| |||||||||| |||||||||| |||||||||| |||||||||| ||||||| **76%**
|||||||||| |||||||||| |||||||||| |||||||||| |||||||||| |||||||||| || **62%**
My company's relationship with its customers will be stronger in five years

|||||||||| |||||||||| |||||||||| |||||||||| |||||||||| |||||||||| |||||| || **72%**
|||||||||| |||||||||| |||||||||| |||||||||| |||||||||| || **56%**
My company will be using the latest technology to provide better experiences for customers in five years

|||||||||| |||||||||| |||||||||| |||||||||| |||||||||| |||||||||| || **70%**
|||||||||| |||||||||| |||||||||| |||||||||| **39%**
My company will be more innovative than other firms in our industry or category over the next five years

|||||||||| |||||||||| |||||||||| |||||||||| |||||||||| **50%**
|||||||||| |||||||||| |||||||||| |||||||||| |||||||||| |||||||||| **59%**
It is very likely that companies outside of our industry will have an easier time using digital tools and experiences to change our industry than for companies currently inside our industry

|||||||||| |||||||||| |||||||||| |||||||||| |||||||||| |||||||||| |||||||||| |||**73%**
|||||||||| |||||||||| |||||||||| |||||||||| |||||||||| |||||||||| | **61%**
People in our company are excited about the changes that digital will bring to our company

|||||||||| |||||||||| |||||||||| |||||||||| |||||||||| ||| **53%**
|||||||||| |||||||||| |||||||||| || **32%**
People in our company have the skills needed to adapt to the changes that digital will bring to our company

|||||||||| |||||||||| |||||||||| |||||||||| |||||||||| **49%**
|||||||||| |||||||||| |||| **24%**
Our company has policies and business practices that will enable us to adapt to the changes that digital will bring to our company

|||||||||| |||||||||| |||||||||| |||||||||| |||||||||| |||||||||| **60%**
|||||||||| |||||||||| |||||| **27%**
Our company will put the right resources (people, budget, time) in place to adapt to the changes that digital will bring to our company

|||||||||| |||||||||| |||||||||| |||||||||| |||||||||| |||||||||| |||||||||| ||| **74%**
|||||||||| |||||||||| |||||||||| |||||||||| ||| **44%**
I am able to navigate my company's policies and business practices to adapt to the changes that digital will bring to our company

Base: 285 global executives invited to participate
Source: Forrester Digital Readiness Assessment, June 2012

In July of 2012, Disney's SVP of social games, John Spinale, spoke at GamesBeat, a gaming conference in San Francisco. There he uttered these powerful words: "Historically, at Disney, we probably haven't done the absolute best job of being a games company. We've started off as a film company, then television, parks, and continuing to broaden out the portfolio of things that we did. But I think games, until pretty recently, was more of an afterthought."[1]

This kind of public frankness is a welcome sign of growth at Disney, growth that I am certain Where's My Water? has helped stimulate. Because after Where's My Water?, Disney took the same basic game and applied it to Perry the Platypus, a beloved character from the hit Disney Channel show *Phineas and Ferb*. The resulting game was called Where's My Perry?, an instant monetization opportunity. That's Disney taking what it had learned from the new experiment and applying it directly— across silos—to new product experiments.

It's also encouraging to see that Disney has partnered with Imangi Studios, a mobile gaming company that is technically a competitor.[2] Maker of the fabulously popular Temple Run mobile game, Imangi created the perfect opportunity for Disney to take its own disruption one step further. If developing a hit game with internal resources is one way to quickly get a hit to market, what would happen if the company partnered with an existing hit-maker to adapt its bestselling game to fit Disney's needs? And thus Temple Run: Brave, was born, a ninety-nine-cent version of the game featuring the lead character from the newest Disney/Pixar movie *Brave*. The game quickly shot to the top of the paid game list in the App Store.

And so we have, in less than one year, three very successful mobile games from one of the world's largest media companies, a company that had historically struggled to leave its mark on this emerging game platform. All three games were brought to life through disruptive processes that required thinking differently, working differently, and even partnering differently.

As we welcome Disney to the world of digital disruption, we sincerely wish to welcome you, too. You really can do this. You just have to know what steps to take next.

9

Your Path to Digital Disruption

You know what a digital disruptor is and you know why you have to become one. You know how ready you, your team, and your company are to begin the digital disruption process. What you need now is a plan. In this chapter, I give you specific steps you can take to disrupt yourself before someone else can do it to you. You will digitally disrupt your *process* in order to digitally disrupt your *product* experience.

In September of 2006, two Brown University alums, Benjamin Rubin and Paolo DePetrillo, introduced the product that would become known as Zeo: an alarm clock that included a sensor-enabled wireless headband that monitors sleep. Zeo was designed to track a sleeper's brain waves, identifying shifts between sleep phases, transition points at which research has shown people awaken feeling more refreshed. The device can trigger an alarm, waking the wearer at precisely the right moment to maximize their readiness for the day's events. By innovating the adjacent possible, the Zeo's creators have since taken on many other consumer needs with the device, providing a range of sleep-related diagnostics and benefits.

Engineering students from Brown came up with Zeo after a fellow student complained about performing poorly on an exam due to waking up feeling unrefreshed. That's no surprise. But what may surprise you is that major healthcare companies, major medical institutions, and other experts in the field of sleep science didn't beat them to it.

Zeo Inc. has attracted millions of investor dollars. That's because, according to Zeo CEO Dave Dickinson, there are probably 113 million people in America that fit into the "sleep concerned" category. These people experience less than ideal sleep for any number of reasons ranging from health issues to lifestyle choices. Of the total, an estimated sixty-four million suffer from a diagnosable condition that inhibits effective sleep. Of those people, Dickinson estimates that no more than 10 percent have been diagnosed and treated.

Do the math and you have an undiagnosed fifty-seven million people who need significant help to sleep better, plus another fifty million who could benefit at least somewhat from improved sleep. Today, major pharmaceutical firms, insurance companies, and healthcare practitioners help most of these people through medication, a risk-laden and terribly expensive way to address a symptom that ignores what may be crucial underlying causes. Inadequate sleep is a killer: People who do not get sufficient rest are significantly more susceptible to many major illnesses. And it's a marker of other potential problems including mood disorders, many of which first manifest as sleep trouble.

Today, medical professionals often diagnose sleep problems at sleep centers where patients go to sleep under observation, hooked up to a variety of sensors and apparatuses. The sleep center experts diagnose and recommend solutions for major sleep problems. But the majority of us will never consider spending a night in a sleep center because our problems with sleep are not significant enough (or so we think), because obtaining insurance coverage or a referral is too difficult, or because the effort required to follow through on a visit is just too onerous.

But this calculus changes when there's a $100 Zeo headband that provides insight into how well we're sleeping and can identify behaviors and events in our waking hours that undermine or aid our sleep. If Zeo can carefully identify, say, just ten million of the more than one hundred million people with untreated sleep concerns—those whose fundamental need for comfort aligns with this unique approach to addressing sleep problems—the company could theoretically sell ten million units in short order, putting it at the level of adoption of devices like Amazon's Kindle in its first few years.

So why did neither the Mayo Clinic, Blue Cross Blue Shield, nor Pfizer choose to develop and deploy this technology? Because they failed to ask and answer three simple questions: How, who, and what. In this case, these companies did not ask themselves: How do we prepare ourselves to disruptively see and then act on the next thing our customers need? Who do we need to track, build a relationship with, and anticipate needs for? And what would our new product experience look like?

These companies—like yours—are busy doing their daily tasks. They each have their metrics, they each have their mission statements tacked up on a wall somewhere, and they each have a process for getting the job done. Major medical institutions like the Mayo Clinic are organized to save lives, not to seek opportunities for disruption; as a result, they don't see even obvious opportunities to engage in it. Insurers like any one of the Blue Cross Blue Shield companies have all of their customers in databases, but there's no field in that database called "unmet needs," leaving them to efficiently record customer interactions while ignoring opportunities to anticipate their adjacent possibilities. Major drug companies like Pfizer invest in and distribute critical medications but they have no concept of what a total product experience—around those medications or something as peripheral as a Zeo headband—might look like.

For lack of answers to these three questions, billion-dollar companies were not organized to look for the Zeo opportunity, did not have a customer relationship that would have led them to it, and still have yet to identify a way that Zeo could improve their own total product experience today.

Digital disruption doesn't happen at many companies, large or small, for lack of answers to these three questions. Companies don't know how to disrupt themselves, who they're disrupting for, or what that disruption should look like.

You're more likely to be in the situation of the healthcare companies and sleep centers trying not to be disrupted than to be Zeo. But there is a Zeo in your industry waiting to disrupt you—in fact, as I pointed out in chapter 1, there are probably hundreds of them. The only alternative is to do it to yourself first. You have to unleash this wave of digital disruption from within your own company. How?

You need to answer three questions: How, who, and what. How can we disrupt ourselves? Who are we disrupting for? What should that disruption look like? These three questions tie together all the information covered so far in the book, centralizing the action imperatives from all the previous chapters into a single opportunity for you to craft your digital-disruption plan. You'll recognize each of the concepts I present in this chapter, but you'll see how they become not only doable but also more powerful when organized into a single plan. First, a look at how they all tie together:

How? Digitally disrupt yourself. Show that you have adopted a digital disruptor's mindset by revamping your policies and practices.

1. Establish digital disruption as a C-level priority
2. dentify and plan to route around all silo barriers to digital disruption
3. Designate small innovation teams to identify disruptive opportunities
4. Make all indirect competition explicit and learn from it

Who? Start with your customer. Build customer-focused skills that prepare you to develop a new product experience.

1. Identify the fundamental customer needs you do/should meet
2. Put yourself in your customer's shoes and ask what benefits they want next
3. Construct a list of adjacent possibilities for your customer and identify those that are possibilities for your company

What? Create total product experiences. Build the next big experience, but do so faster and more cheaply than before.

1. Build a digital bridge into your product experience
2. Use totally free, nearly free, or essentially free digital tools
3. Partner promiscuously
4. Measure differently
5. Accept and expect failure

Let's get into this advice in more detail.

How? Digitally Disrupt Yourself

Show that you have adopted a digital disruptor's mindset by revamping your policies and practices. In the last chapter, we identified that policies and practices are the Achilles' heel of companies' digital ambitions. That's why process is the first step in digital disruption: Before you can disrupt your product, you have to disrupt your process. This happens in four steps:

1. **Establish digital disruption as a C-level priority.** As our survey showed, few C-level executives believe that they are failing to take digital seriously. But do lower-down employees in the company believe that the C-level executives understand digital and are ready to prioritize it? In one company I work with, the CEO went to great pains in his meetings with other senior executives to communicate that digital was priority one across the company. But feedback continued to reach him that people were uncertain and concerned. Finally, as part of a two-day series of workshops, the company had me present to more than two hundred people in their marketing organization. The CEO came to these meetings to kick off the workshops and to personally endorse the process. I have never seen two hundred people take a workshop that seriously.

Don't just shout from the top—repeat the message frequently. How often does your company hear threatening or worrisome messages about your industry's ability to keep up with the changes that digital will bring? And by comparison, how often does the C-suite offer evidence that it has the matter well in hand? Once a year at a big retreat? Once a quarter as part of an end-of-quarter rally? Even if it's once a month, the number of worrisome messages will certainly outnumber the messages that suggest the company is unprepared for digital.

Companies should also designate a senior executive with formal responsibility for digital. When Random House CEO Markus Dohle enticed former employee Madeline McIntosh to return from Amazon to lead the company's digital efforts, he made her COO of the company rather than giving her a specialized title like chief digital officer. This was powerful both symbolically and in practical terms. Sure, anointing her CDO might have indicated Random House was ready to take digital seriously, but making her COO clearly indicated that the entire company was going to take digital seriously, rather than turn pet digital projects over to a single arm of the company.

2. **Identify and plan to route around all silo barriers to digital disruption.** Here's the ideal version of this: Get the executives together, probably at one of their regular meetings. Then, org chart in hand, identify the barriers between departments that stand in the way of digital disruption—legal and finance approvals, regional sales structures, or gaps between engineering and marketing—that create a culture of "their fault" whenever things go wrong. Let people be honest without encouraging them to whine. That's the way it should work. I have only seen this kind of meeting—with all the senior executives in the company present—twice. Both times it was painful and only once was the result overwhelmingly positive. In the other case, it was a necessary but insufficient first step.

So how do you get this job done if you can't do it the ideal way? I've seen it work effectively in the context of a single high-priority project. If, say, an insurance company wants to completely revamp the claims process, the executives in charge can use the mandate they have been given to diagnose the silo barriers to digital disruption in that context. The goal here is still to identify the blockages in the flow of innovation, so you can plan how you'll handle those bottlenecks. Are there cross-functional roles that need to be established? Is there a C-level intervention that can resolve differences? Can the company work on the issues across teams to identify possible process solutions? For example, in the previous chapter I described a consumer products manufacturer where the CMO came out of the product engineering team and had a very clear understanding of the ways that product engineering and marketing could work together but usually did not. As a result, he designed an innovation flow that would allow each team to do what it did best, while preserving the accountability of each division so that at no point could one side bail on a project and point the finger at the other side.

3. **Designate small innovation teams to identify disruptive opportunities.** If you already have teams that are pounding down the door of upper management, asking for approval to try new ideas, start with them. If you don't, issue a call for the best ideas for digital disruption in any corner of the company. Spend less time evaluating the actual ideas and more time evaluating which teams or departments generated the most unexpected and insightful suggestions. Look for enthusiasm as a marker of the energy and motivation that those teams will bring to the task. Then ask the teams that show the most promise to identify small subteams to work not only on refining their prior ideas, but on generating as many additional ideas as they can.

   With C-level support in place, these teams will have the confidence to propose the best ideas regardless of what other silos will feel the impact. Related teams may even get inspired by the work of their colleagues. The principal source of excitement in these cases is the hope that they might soon be given the freedom to do some innovating on their own. If executives clearly state that this is the case, it will help defuse the silo-based infighting in which each team roots for the failure of others in hopes that resources will be freed up for them to have a go at it. In Disney's case, as Tim FitzRandolph's team succeeded, other teams also received the green light to pursue related disruptions because the company was savoring the taste of digitally disruptive success and was getting an appetite for pursuing more of it.

Small teams are critical at this point because they have to be nimble. Amazon CTO Werner Vogels famously said its project teams should never be bigger than you could feed with two large pizzas.[1] While there is no specific team configuration that is ideal in every situation, big teams struggle to bear the burden of their own weight. They can't even schedule a meeting because so many people have to sync up their calendars. They can't move forward because they have to listen to everyone's internal opinions instead of listening to the customer's needs. To avoid these problems, start smaller rather than larger—the number five stands out from my interview with Tim at Disney—and add expertise if you need it.

4. **Make all indirect competition explicit and learn from it.** Who are your new competitors? Start with a list of the usual suspects: companies in your industry that offer a competing product experience. Now put that list to the side and work on the really important list. Ask yourself who else is doing interesting things in the product area you're innovating—like Zeo in health care. Look for substitution opportunities: If your customer were no longer able to acquire your product or use your service, where else would they turn? Think as widely as possible on this one.

While major retailers were busy competing with each other to create full-body-scanning dressing rooms for their retail environments, complete with expensive imaging cameras, many failed to notice that the new video game accessory invented by Microsoft could do the same job with a technology provided by a company like FaceCake. They weren't on the lookout for Microsoft as a competitor or a partner because they were in continual talks with dressing room-imaging vendors. When FaceCake appeared, retailers realized they'd been looking at the wrong competitors. This step fits under the *How* because these competitors, direct as well as indirect, will often show your own organization what is possible. Their differences in size and organization can help motivate you to revamp policies and practices as needed to compete with them rather than falling back on the silo-based thinking that blocks you now.

Who? Start with Your Customer

Build customer skills that prepare you to develop a new product experience. Once your organization has adopted a disruptor's mindset and revamped its policies and practices to stimulate digital disruption, it has to bow to and commit to the service of the end customer. Even though this section starts with *Who*, no longer is it sufficient to ask "Who is the right customer for our products?" Instead, you must train yourselves, over and over, to think, "What is the right product *experience* for our *current or desired* customer?"

1. **Identify the fundamental customer needs you meet or should meet.** When Jawbone product managers set out to create the next product for the company, they reduced their understanding of their customer to the most fundamental unit they could. Instead of describing their customer as a combination of demographics and behaviors, they expressed the essence of that customer by saying it was someone who aspired to a

mobile lifestyle. This was a challenging but attainable segment, one the company has successfully targeted and captured with the Jambox line of mobile speakers.

Jawbone says its customers "aspire to a mobile lifestyle." In terms of our needs framework—comfort, connection, uniqueness, and variety—aspiration is a desire for uniqueness, the ability to set oneself apart from others in ways that have meaning to the individual. This is the primary fundamental need the company targets, building in features and experiences that address the other three needs through the adjacent possible.

The typical company lacks this understanding of the consumer needs they are fulfilling. I once spent several days with one of the world's largest consumer electronics makers. They were pleased to show me that they had developed a complex customer segmentation model that was needs-based. As we walked through the segmentation and their excitement mounted, mine evaporated. Their definition of needs was behavior-based. They believed that one segment "needed" to watch movies with the whole family while another "needed" to watch TV shows alone. These are not needs, they are behaviors, and the end result of the segmentation was that—surprise!—they discovered that there were exactly the right number of people in each segment to explain their historical sales patterns for their line of TVs.

That same company has struggled with its market share ever since. It's not the segmentation's fault, certainly, but the segmentation clearly didn't help where it could have. Because it had been designed to confirm the behaviors customers had shown in the past, it was unable to prepare the company to understand how behavior might change in the future as consumers find new ways to meet their fundamental needs.

When in doubt, return to the fundamental needs of your customers and ask, "What do they really need?" Dive into the psychology of your customers, drawing on whatever combination of data and gut instinct you have to ask, "How are they meeting those needs with us today?" Do they come to you more for comfort or variety? Once you know what needs they currently turn to you to fulfill, ask the most important questions, "How else will they meet those needs in the future?" and "What other needs could we fulfill in the same product experience?"

2. **Put yourself in your customers' shoes and ask what benefits they want *next*.** Needs are fundamental and therefore vague. So your customer wants comfort. Now what? Translate the fundamental need into a benefit statement. Let's start with an example from Nordstrom, where they were selling sunglasses. Here's how they could have thought about it (although, as you'll see, they didn't):

> Need: Our customer needs a higher degree of uniqueness than the average person.

> Benefit: Therefore, they will benefit from our line of premium sunglasses because they are distinctive and stylish.

Here's why this is wrong: A line of premium sunglasses may be stylish and distinctive, but that doesn't automatically benefit the customer. These are product features, not benefits. Let's rewrite this as a good example:

> Need: Our customer needs a higher degree of uniqueness than the average person.

> Benefit: Therefore, they will seek sunglasses that are visibly distinctive and recognized by others as stylish.

Why this is a good example: The difference appears subtle at first, but it's a critical one. Are your sunglasses just stylish or are they recognizably stylish? How can you convey the difference to your customer? Large racks of sunglasses on the retail floor may communicate variety to the customer, but they also make it hard to perceive any single set of frames as unique. Is there a digitally disruptive way to help people isolate the most distinctive looks and begin to attach themselves to that look in a way that reinforces their need for uniqueness?

Nordstrom approached exactly this question in a very direct way. The company's developer lab placed a team inside a flagship store at the sunglasses department for a week to dive directly into the needs of consumers, developing a digital app experience that would deliver benefits. But which benefits? You can actually watch the team's development process on YouTube.[2] There you'll see how the team started with an assumption about what benefits such an app should provide, starting with the ability to capture an image of a customer in a pair of sunglasses to help him or her evaluate the look. They then combined feedback from internal sales staff as well as customers trying to buy sunglasses, which led them to add features step by step, addressing what those constituents each needed next, such as the ability to perform side-by-side comparisons of two or more captured images.

By putting itself in the customer's shoes on the retail floor, this team built an app that helps people find the perfect—and perfectly unique—pair of sunglasses amid a sea of frames competing for attention. The exercise demonstrates perfectly how to iteratively ask what benefits your customer wants next and investing those benefits back into the product experience to meet fundamental needs.

3. **Construct a list of adjacent possibilities for your customer, then identify those that are possibilities for your company.** Understanding what benefits your customer wants next will lead you to generate a list of adjacent possibilities you can consider providing. Don't fall into the trap of incremental versus ideal innovation, as we described in chapter 6.

Simply let the customer's needs and benefits be your guide. Make the list long and robust, even dare to include ridiculous things that you know aren't feasible—you can learn from infeasible options as much as you can the feasible ones.

However, when it comes time to determine which possibilities to pursue, you will have to say no to most of them. Many brainstorms I've participated in accomplish this by formally attacking the list and trying to discredit the obvious losers. This is dangerous. Psychologically it sets the wrong tone, putting people in a mental frame that encourages rejection of scary ideas rather than instilling courage to embrace good ideas. It also opens the door to political maneuvering on the part of people who want to score points, shoot down other teams, or otherwise whine.

Avoid saying no to some projects by simply saying yes to the ones you are most capable of doing and leaving the rest to wait their turn in line for later consideration. Think of it this way. If you generated twelve adjacent possibilities your company could develop in service of your customers' needs, but you only have the resources to pursue two of them, which is the easier task: crossing off ten of them or selecting two of them? Crossing off ten will be rancorous, personal, political, and time-consuming. It will also engage all the parts of the brain that you don't want to cede thinking to. Instead, you should prioritize the top contenders based on their immediate feasibility. How easy is it to develop the idea into a prototype experience and how quickly can we test whether that prototype will meet consumer needs? A decision process based on these questions will keep the focus squarely set on the consumer, draw on the parts of the brain that are good at attacking problems with creative solutions, and avoid the sticky political issues involved in the rejection of the other ten ideas.

The CBSP framework from chapter 7—Customer, Benefits, Strategy, Product—can help here. It's the path down which we have helped many companies establish a customer-focused innovation process. It defuses political infighting, engaging the right parts of people's brains so they dive in and readily suggest adjacent possibilities that can be developed into new product experiences rather than carving out territory or protecting interests. Even when the time comes for executives to choose which product experiences to put money behind, people are more encouraging of one another than we have anticipated, possibly because they see that senior executive support for good ideas and good processes will eventually lead to opportunities for all good ideas, including theirs, in the future.

What? Create Total Product Experiences

Build the next big experience, but do so more quickly and cheaply. Now that you have digitally disrupted your company and have focused solidly on the needs of your end customer, it's time to give them something. But what? That's where the idea of a total product experience I described in chapter 7 comes in. The end of your digital disruption journey will be a place where your product concept is bigger, more expansive, and more useful than it has ever been before.

1. **Build a digital bridge into your product experience.**
    HBO has twenty-eight million subscribers in the United States alone, although it has no relationship with most of them—it connects with them through cable and satellite providers. But in the digitally disrupted future, not knowing its customers will be a problem, because it's far too easy for others like Hulu, Netflix, and YouTube to take over the online viewing experience. Unfortunately, HBO can't just sell HBO programming to viewers directly, going around its cable and satellite partners, because that would create competition between HBO and its key partners. But if HBO didn't create a customer relationship, it would have no future bridge over which to serve its longstanding and money-spending customers.
    The solution for HBO was HBO GO, an online experience delivered to computers, tablets, and phones that gives HBO

subscribers access to HBO programming. To use it, people must verify that they are paid subscribers through cable or satellite. The solution is smart business on the simple level that it doesn't upset its existing cable and satellite partners. But it's absolutely essential if HBO hopes to be well positioned for the digital disruption that is bearing down on the TV industry. HBO has successfully built a bridge *over* its current partners' heads, creating a direct customer relationship that for the first time gives HBO the opportunity to ask customers a simple but profoundly important question: Who are you?

Now, when millions of HBO customers who have signed up to access the HBO GO apps log in, HBO knows who they are. In fact, this digital bridge is especially important to HBO because not only does it create a new customer relationship, it creates a *two-way* relationship that for the first time reveals mountains of data about how people watch HBO and what they are viewing.

Every product experience can have a digital bridge like this built into it. Consider the toothbrush, a simple product that is one of the least considered products in a consumer's home. But add iPhone-type accelerometers to the toothbrush and you now have a toothbrush that can report on how often and how effectively it is being used. That data is gold for many companies. The toothbrush manufacturer certainly wants that information to know whether the product is providing the benefits promised in the marketing. But the dental insurance company and the dentist should also care. And what about Amazon, the company that wants to sell you all your floss, your toothpaste, and any other bathroom products that might keep you healthy?

Every product experience can have a digital bridge built into it. It's just a question of who will build it and when. What about yours?

2. **Use totally free, nearly free, or essentially free tools.**
   Free tools now power more and more businesses at every scale, whether we're talking about the open-source Hadoop software

that Cloudera and its huge clients use to extract insights from massive customer data files or the mobile phones that every app developer on the planet exploits to get their games, utilities, or other apps in front of consumers.

Are you using free tools? If not, why not? You can rest assured (or rest terrified, more likely) that your competitors, both direct and indirect, are using free tools, for two main reasons. Obviously, as I explained in chapter 3, free tools reduce costs. But they also save time, because they remove the lengthy procurement and vendor selection processes that often stall an idea up front.

There is another reason to use free tools. It energizes innovators to see their ideas translated into practical realities in minutes and seconds, not weeks or months. Continuum Innovation's prototyping labs have every type of material available for rapidly crafting things as varied as electronic credit-card holders and new chairs for medical exams. The people in those labs positively brim with excitement. They're *doing* something, they're *exploring* new ways to provide benefits to their clients' customers.

These days, do-it-yourself chutzpah is common. In fact, one might say it's the engine behind the modern economy. And that's the whole point of digital disruption. When even more tools are emancipated and given to the masses, even more power will be distributed to the people with the best ideas. Will you be one of them? Will your company benefit from these tools or regard them with suspicion?

3. **Partner promiscuously.** In a digitally disruptive era, with free tools powering more companies (including companies far outside of your traditional radar), you have to move quickly. But you can't possibly move quickly if you are required to build everything yourself. Luckily for you, you don't have to. That's why the power of promiscuous partnership is today a source of competitive advantage but will soon be just the cost of doing business.

The company that can rapidly identify the smartest and most effective development, design, manufacturing, distribution, and marketing partners is also the company that will win. This will include partnering intelligently with your most feared competitors as needed to get the job done. Gone are the days of jealously guarding partnerships to ensure that no one involved gets their feelings hurt.

We can learn a lot from digital platform providers in this regard. Amazon uses Google's Android OS to power its Kindle tablets, but it locks out the Google Play App Store. Microsoft will gladly rent you a digital movie on the Xbox 360 through its Zune store, but its Bing search engine on the game console returns the options to watch the same or competing content on Hulu Plus, VUDU, or Netflix. And Amazon would desperately love for you to buy a Kindle HD tablet and become a locked-in Amazon platform customer for life, but not only will the company sell you an iPad, it will also let you download a free Kindle app to that iPad so you can read all your Kindle books on it.

On a smaller scale, we see this same friendly wrestle for customer attention happening in many of the customer experiences we have profiled in this book. The Fitbit activity monitor will tell you how much you move during the day but it also monitors your sleep efficiency and has an interface where you can track your calorie consumption. These are services that Zeo and Lose It! also provide, making them competitors. Yet Fitbit has partnered with both companies so that its customers can access these rival services as part of the Fitbit experience.

This will take some time for people to get used to, especially more experienced executives. In a digital environment, the ability to deliver value to the customer is what matters, not petty practices for establishing and maintaining barriers to competition. A relationship built on locking each other into exclusive and limiting relationships rather than on delivering each other actual value may have worked for the railroad tycoons or big automakers and auto unions, but in a digitally disruptive era, you either deliver value to your customers with the help of partners, or you don't. No need to indulge in golf games at exclusive clubs, dine over linen tablecloths, or smoke big cigars to signal the partners' emotional alignment with one another. Get over it and get on with it.

4. **Measure differently.** Why didn't research hospitals, health insurance providers, pharmaceutical companies, or consumer electronics companies make a product like Zeo? Because they didn't ask the right questions early enough.

Instead, they spend their time and their planning meetings asking a *wrong* question about new initiatives. "What is our expected return on investment?" The calculations behind ROI, including the classic internal rate of return on capital that they teach in business classes, may be useful financial metrics for a company, but they are completely useless when trying to adapt to changing circumstances in an industry.

If Disney had insisted on asking Tim FitzRandolph to demonstrate that he could achieve a certain level of return, there is no way he would have gotten the green light to develop Where's My Water?. In fact, one of the main reasons that most digital disruptors are in startups is that startups don't have historical rates of return to consider. And in today's maximally disruptive, low-capital digital startup environment, many of these startups don't even have to ask for venture capital, thus avoiding any arbitrary rate of return calculation imposed on them by the venture capitalists.

For digitally disruptive initiatives, replace ROI with ROD, or *return on disruption*. Where the goal in ROI is to generate a known return from a known investment, the goal in ROD is to invest as little as possible, placing quick, cheap bets on the initiatives with the largest possible breakout success. Spend zero time trying to prove how likely that success is. Instead, go try to make it happen, one adjacent step at a time. Because the costs are low, you can afford to aim for the right success rather than the likely success, confident that you'll learn from your effort even if you don't achieve the targeted success.

5. **Accept and expect failure.** It's human nature. People presented with uncertain business decisions stall in whatever way they can. They ask for more information, they blame inaction on the other department, they say they don't have sufficient resources, or they say the tools IT has given them are inadequate. This is not because they are incompetent. It is because they are afraid to fail.

Senior-level executives love to talk about bold innovation and taking risks. Yet senior managers at large companies are among the most risk-averse people in business. That risk aversion is precisely what makes them useful as managers of large corporate budgets and divisions. But because of that, everyone reporting to them knows that although they talk big and they frequently assert that the company is ready to innovate, you can't really get a proposal past those individuals because they will vigorously guard against any failure on their watch.

After a recent speech in the UK, where many managers are highly risk-averse, one of the audience members asked me for advice on how to accept and expect failure. It was an honest question and there were nervous looks in the room. I took the opportunity to ask the room of fifty or sixty people to indicate by a show of hands how many of their managers and senior executives claim to be willing to fail, to learn from their mistakes. Most hands went up.

"Now keep your hand up if you think they really mean it, that they will thank you if your next innovation fails."

Hands went down. Of course managers don't want to be associated with failed efforts. Digital disruptors don't either. It's not that they revel in dead-ends, it's just that digital disruptors understand that finding your way through an uncharted wilderness requires starting down a few of those dead ends—like Lose It! and its initially ill-designed social features. That's why digital disruptors keep the scope of their innovations small. Rather than creating a five-year innovation plan that shoots for the ideal innovation, digital disruptors proceed from adjacent possibility to adjacent possibility, occasionally failing, but failing so quickly and so cheaply that recovery can be nearly immediate.

————

There you have it, a list of next steps you can take to plan your path to digital disruption. You move from *How* to *Who* to *What*, at each step preparing not for a single or point outcome but instead preparing to be a company that engages in these steps in perpetuity, accelerating the move from step to step, tweaking and improving as needed within these principles with an eye steadfastly fixed on the end customer.

As you can see, the outcome is not magical. It's transformative, certainly, but in ways that will feel right and natural when these steps become second nature. That's the thing about the future, it always seems incomprehensible just before you get there, but once you arrive, you feel as though you are right at home.

And you will arrive just in time to face the next disruption.

10

The Next Disruption

When companies *adopt* technology, they do old things in new ways. When companies *internalize* technology, the find entirely new—disruptive—things to do. You must move from merely using technology to get the job done to disrupting yourself and your market by depending on, exploiting, and pushing the boundaries of technology. Act on what you've learned in this book and you will be well on your way. But recognize that there's an even more profound disruption yet to come, because:

When companies adopt disruption, they do old things in disruptive new ways. When companies internalize disruption, they advance to the next level, they initiate the next disruption.

Start by admitting that you cannot imagine what your product, your service, or even your internal process will look like in five years, because technology will continually reshape your market, hopefully with your digitally disruptive guidance.

But technology is ultimately just a tool here, a tool in the hands of digital disruptors who share a mindset that feels new to us today. What if it weren't new? Just as today's teenagers grew up in an internet-enabled world and will do things in that world that we older folks strain to imagine, the next generation of disruptors will have grown up in a world where digital disruption was the order of the day. They will know nothing else.

And taking to it like a fish to water, they will dramatically alter every industry in the world.

The rules of the game as we play it today, even modified to account for digital disruption, will not suffice for the next generation of disruptors. They will make new rules and they will barely know they are doing it. We can see hints of those rules in the kinds of experiences emerging now, both on the consumer side and the business side. With that in mind, here are five rules of the next disruption, a truly new way to do business.

1. The Power of One

Power in the industrial economy was achieved through scale. The larger the company, the more it could do. The bigger the labor base, the greater the strength of the company—the more products it could make, the more widely it could distribute them, and the more leverage it could wield over business partners and customers. Assuming this would always be true, companies hired more people and developed policies and practices designed to retain them for extended periods. Following this model, Pfizer employs more than one hundred thousand people, IBM employs nearly half a million, and Walmart employs more than two million individuals around the world.

But now it is no longer true that size of company matters. This is not because larger companies have a harder time innovating in digitally disruptive ways. What matters most is how much you can multiply the power of each individual employee by using digital tools and by exploiting digital platforms. The employees that deliver the most value will be those who make contributions that can be multiplied digitally.

This shifts the nature and balance of power in the work world. As Daniel Pink identified a decade ago in his book *Free Agent Nation*, in extremely talent-driven industries like sports, companies already must manage employee talent differently than in other industries.[1] Today we see this extending to other talent-dependent fields like investment banking and software development, where employees may be more valuable than the companies they work for. Since the beginning of this decade, companies like Amazon and Microsoft have had to pay software developers as much as three hundred thousand dollars a year to keep them employed. Why so much? Because the stock those companies used to offer developers can't even begin to compare with the value these employees deliver—and many of those employees know they could leave and become digital disruptors at any company, or on their own.

This phenomenon will expand, reaching far beyond the industries it affects today. This will lead to the rise of a new employment model—call it the mercenary model—in which the norms of what we currently call employment will evaporate. Employers will borrow from the Hollywood model, where above-the-line talent work for themselves, represented by talent agencies and hired out to complete specific, defined tasks. This model will include flexible work arrangements in which a consulting firm may "hire" a mercenary to join their team to pitch a large implementation at a Fortune 100 company. But the mercenary may also pitch services to that same company directly, or to a competing outsourced consulting firm. All this will happen without formal employment agreements as we define them today.

The upshot of this is that individual power will expand, at least for the next disruptors.

2. Living a Data-mined Life

The barrier to free agency reaching into more types of roles across more industries is the high cost of coordinating relationships between employers and mercenary employees. Companies prefer to hire people as full-time employees because it's easier to work with a stable base of employees than to have to constantly sift through the available talent pool to match the right person to the right task. There's too much uncertainty for a company to risk making a bad match. And mercenaries have no easy way to tell prospective clients what they can do, or what they ought to charge for it. The next disruption will fix that inefficiency.

I expect to see the rise of services that operate like Moody's, but focused on ranking and valuing individuals in their performance. These services will use not just direct feedback by colleagues and clients—as we already see in LinkedIn—but also digital metrics that workers' own technology will collect from them as they work. Mercenaries will agree to contribute this information, because a pool of data about one's own performance will enable potential clients to find them in a simple search. This is the next, more sophisticated step beyond the keyword-based resume search tactics people use to hire now.

Data could come from any device a mercenary uses. Apps will follow their performance throughout the day, counting things like the minutes they spend in calls, the level and prestige of the people they deal with over email, not to mention the complexity and influence of their social networks. Workers eager to get more ratings will log in to the ratings system on all their various computers and tablets, which will track how quickly they go from first draft to finished work. When coupled with performance scores submitted by their collaborators, these ratings systems will be able to score them on new metrics like work satisfaction delivered per minute of effort.

The next disruptors enroll in this system because it will reduce the friction that inhibits connecting them with the best projects and because it will ensure that they spend less time looking for work and more time doing it. But they'll also do it because the system will track data in both directions. Just as prospective hiring companies will be able to sort through disruptors to find the ones best suited to the tasks they have on their docket, the disruptors will have the ability to evaluate similarly crucial data about their prospective employers, even identifying their likely fit with the team leaders inside the organization that they'll report to.

Not everyone will enroll in this system, just as not everyone uses Twitter today. But the *best* disruptors will. And disadvantaged by our unwillingness to reveal our stats to prospective clients, others of us will gradually give in, participating more and more each year. It may have taken a while, but you probably eventually joined LinkedIn because your colleagues and contacts were there. The same dynamic will apply here.

3. Share and Share Alike

During the next disruption, these disruptors will have such confidence in their newfound success that they will undo one of the most enduring tenets of economics: scarcity. Partly because the next disruptors will have been weaned on free things, they will assume that every good fruit hanging from the digital tree is infinitely renewable. The next disruptors will look back at the rest of us as barbarians who clung too tightly to what will seem like small and miserly ways.

If something can't be exhausted, it can be shared without penalty. In fact, to the next disruptor, it should be. This isn't wishful thinking; I heard this principle repeated in most of my interviews. Jeff Hammerbacher, chief data scientist at Cloudera, is a good example. In the middle of our interview about his company's use of open-source software to mine massive datasets for new insights, he casually referred to data science classes he had volunteered to teach in the computer science program at Berkeley, the entire curriculum of which he makes available for free online for anyone who aspires to become a data scientist. I asked him why was he teaching classes and giving away his knowledge to the world in what is certainly precious spare time.

"I'm very sensitive to the fact that I have a finite amount of time on this earth. I don't subscribe to the 'great man' theory of the world. I'd much rather create fertile soil for other innovators to plant their seeds in than just water my own tree."

As a digital disruptor who has built his business on free software, Jeff has not only accepted that sharing is a good thing, he has decided it is imperative. Not just because it feels good, but because it makes everybody else smarter. And those smarter people, whether they end up as future collaborators or competitors, end up benefiting the whole community.

For the next disruptors, this lesson of their own experience will be clear: There will be ample, even accelerating, knowledge. The more we share, the more we all have to work with, the more disruptive we are, the better off we all are.

Remember Thomas Suarez, the thirteen-year-old developer from chapter 1? Consider again what he said: "A lot of kids these days like to play games. But now they want to make them. And it's difficult, because not many kids know where to go to find out how to make a program. I mean, for soccer, you could go to a soccer team, for violin, you could get lessons for a violin. But what if you want to make an app? Where do you go to find out how to make an app?"

His answer was to teach them. He didn't evaluate the business model of teaching other kids how to code, he didn't run through the ROI of sharing his knowledge to determine whether it would net him any benefit in the long run, he simply shared because that's the way the next disruptors think, that's what they do. It's what Jeff does by volunteering to teach free classes at Berkeley, it's what Gabrielle (aka Design Mom) does when she opens up her server logs and teaches other bloggers how to get more comments, more advertisers, and more traffic.

And it's what you'll do, too. If you want to be relevant, that is.

4. The Disposable Company

I've just predicted that the next disruption will completely disassemble two of the most fundamental sources of corporate value: a proprietary labor pool and intellectual property. But what is a company worth if it can't amass and control those two resources? That is exactly the question the next disruptors will ask. These disruptors will envision new kinds of companies, each type serving whatever purposes are necessary for the conditions at hand.

There will still be giant companies like Disney where a collection of employees creating intellectual property work pretty much as they do now. And there will still be nimble startups, like FitNow. But there will emerge a new type of company I call the disposable company, an entity that exists solely to accomplish a particular task defined by its collaborators. Accelerated by the new labor model where such a company can rapidly scale up, drawing on mercenary employees with whom they will have no permanent relationship, these companies will assemble to serve a particular need, serve that need, and then dispose of the company.

There are intimations of this in the story of FerroKin BioSciences. Dr. Hugh Rienhoff started the company to attack a single molecule and develop it for medical use. He added home-based employees around the world as needed to expand the capabilities of the company, but wherever possible he simply contracted with vendors specializing in particular roles, such as medical trial management or regulatory compliance. When the company achieved its purposes, it was sold to the highest bidder and the contributors—the employees—profited.

Take this model further and you have the disposable company. Imagine that instead of raising tens of millions through traditional sources of venture capital or seed investment, the company was funded by an open market like Kickstarter, with a real-time dashboard that reports the progress of the effort. Rather than raise all the money up front in exchange for equity as a single event, the disposable company will float perpetually on this open market, open to new investment at any time potential collaborators see that value is increasing, routing around securities law by avoiding all the structures that trigger current regulations. Cash will be just one of the ways people can contribute. Some will offer to fulfill roles in the company in exchange for some sort of upside, while others will offer their vendor services or other collaborative input in order to accelerate the project, increase its likelihood of success, and ensure their payout if it succeeds.

Built to dissolve, disposable companies will never seek permanence or durability. Instead, they will actively seek their own dissolution, evaluating their success based not on how long they can survive or how big they can become, but by how quickly they can deliver new value and then enable their employees and contributors to reap the benefits of their contribution and move on to the next thing.

5. Regulation Becomes Obsolete

Consider any of these rules of the next disruption and you quickly realize that even if people are willing to live by them, governments won't be. At least not any government bound by chains of bureaucracy, advantage-seeking politicians, and legal mindsets that predate the Industrial Revolution—which is currently all of them.

The disposable company breaks every rule in the security and investment regulatory framework. Even the very idea that a company is more concerned with its output than its own longevity renders irrelevant most of the regulations that discipline companies with penalties that presume their owners want to cultivate a long-term asset. Governments will try to regulate how people can invest in disposable companies by insisting on the filing of prospectuses, as in an IPO. But the real-time digital metrics delivered by aggregating the actual performance data of the company's employees will be far more informative—not to mention dynamic—than any set of legal forms could be.

Lawyers will object to a share-and-share-alike business philosophy. They will continue to believe that isolation and control of knowledge is the source of value. They will insist on applying copyright law, patent law, and other conventions to compel the next disruptors to behave like good economic citizens—from the 1950s. But the next disruptors will not just disagree, they fundamentally won't get it. When their own experience teaches them that sharing multiplies value, they will find the miserly ways of intellectual property lawyers, patent mongers, and old-school executives inadequate. But rather than flout them by raiding the knowledge of others, they will simply share the knowledge they have with other share-minded disruptors. We see this already emerging in the Creative Commons system for free sharing among disruptive types. But the next disruptors will share even more freely than that, not just seeking recognition for but genuine multiplication of their ideas. Those who refuse to join will find their own knowledge shrivels up and dies because it isn't strengthened by interaction with and multiplication by the knowledge of others.

Transitioning to the data-mined life will be one of the most contentious aspects of the shift to the next disruption, as people take sides on whether the collection and strategic sharing of our private data is fundamentally good or evil. Government agencies will offer to solve the problem by adding regulatory burdens to the process of collecting, analyzing, and distributing data. But the next disruptors will simply not care. Not because they're the free-thinking exhibitionists Facebook users are often accused of being, but because there will be far too much value to be gained from the collecting and sharing of their data.

This all leads back to the power of one. Except in dictatorial regimes or totalitarian states, most participants in the digital economy have the right to decide how to manage all of these things themselves. An individual can choose to broadcast his or her own data within private networks like Facebook or LinkedIn or whatever social network rises to take their place. An individual can choose to raise or invest capital through Kickstarter instead of a formal IPO. An individual can choose to join a loosely confederated group of collaborators to solve a market problem with the aim of disposing of the company as soon as it has reached its goals.

The power of one does not require that the next disruptors *protest* regulation, instead, it dictates that the next disruptors will simply exercise their individual rights and *ignore* regulation.

———

If this scares you, it's because you're not one of the next disruptors, not yet. None of us really are. The next disruptors will do all of this with no second thoughts, relishing in their own improved fortunes by living in the next disruption. It's a power that goes far beyond "doing business." These next disruptors will employ similar philosophies and systems in their personal lives.

We can even project their behavior into a likely, maximally disruptive scenario. Imagine that, sooner than you're prepared to think, these disruptors could use personal monitoring technology to capture and graph trends in things like their vocal patterns, identifying when they were irritable with loved ones, or when they didn't assert themselves enough in their personal relationships. Such individuals would subscribe to personal improvement apps that analyze everything from the nutrition content of their meals to the spring in their step to pre-identify depressive episodes and suggest reliable steps to counteract them before they get in the way of everyday life. Marriage advice could come from an app that taps into in-home 3D cameras and microphones and analyzes patterns in the relationship over the course of several weeks rather than in a series of sit-down office visits. The app would diagnose with statistical precision the likelihood that the relationship will fail if changes aren't made. It would also know exactly which changes to suggest in order to improve the odds and will be able to listen to interactions over the coming weeks to see if the suggestions are being implemented.

There are business opportunities here. The next Oprah to arise in such a scenario would not be an advice-giver and general well-wisher visible in mass media; instead, the Oprah to come would be a guru who helps disruptors tap into all of their data streams and teaches the masses—through personalized interactive apps, of course, with a few high-profile public events to keep loyal fans connected—how to improve every aspect of their lives. And the fans would respond by sharing back to Oprah 2.0 their actual results versus what was predicted by the system, allowing the guru to tune the algorithms and adjust as needed, always proclaiming each new algorithmic insight as a value delivered from the community, back to the community.[2]

This scenario—or the myriad other outcomes the next disruptors will comfortably adopt—is no utopia. In fact, the next disruption will cause some massive problems of its own, such as mind-bending privacy debacles and legal challenges from those who want to preserve the past rather than join the future. But the next disruption will contain within itself the power to identify and fix such problems more rapidly, while providing the incentive for individuals to believe that they have the power to play a role. And they'll play that role not only because they want to solve their own problems but because they'll believe that we can generally contribute to one another's positive outcomes, whether personal or commercial, by sharing knowledge, learning from collectively examined lives, and reducing the artificial sources of friction left over from our analog past. When we're living in the next disruption—when all of us are digital disruptors of a sort—we'll more easily subscribe to the notion expressed by Jeff Hammerbacher when he quipped, "Equipping a wider range of people with a better set of tools is better than trying to build my own jetpack."

In my mind, I can place myself back on that stage in 1999 when I first introduced the world to what I called the digital consumer. We have come a long way since then. Digital consumers, once an exotic breed that we could scarcely comprehend, are now the de facto consumers in the developed world and their behaviors are rapidly spreading into the rest of the world. Companies have had to adapt by learning to use the web, then social media, then mobile platforms, thinking at each step that they were keeping up. But as I've shown in this book, digital consumers and their digital lives add up to much more than any single channel disruption would suggest. Their rapid acceptance of their newfound digital power has stimulated the release of free tools and has led to the rise of digital platforms. All of this has opened the door to the ascent of digital disruptors—digital consumers who have ascended to the next level, using digital tools as a means of production rather than simply as a means of consumption.

Those digital disruptors are rewriting the rules of business. Soon, we will all be them, and when we are, digital disruption will no longer be a phenomenon to examine and analyze , it will just be the way we live.

It's a life worth living. The faster we get there, the better. The sooner you start, the better equipped you will be to fully participate.

See you there.

What's Next?

Wondering how to act on what you've just read? Here are some things you can do next:

- **Get help.** We'd be happy to work with you and your company on strategy and execution for digital disruption. We offer sessions and workshops on analyzing your customers' digital behavior, embracing digital disruption, and innovating the adjacent possible. Learn more and contact us at http://www.forrester.com/DDhelp.
- **Get a speech.** I love speaking to events and companies about digital disruption. To line up a speech, contact us at speakersbureau@forrester.com.
- **Get connected and learn more.** We've got interactive resources for digital disruptors at the website for the book: http://www.forrester.com/disruption. Or you can follow my blog at http://forr.com/DDBLOG and my Twitter at @jmcquivey.

Acknowledgments

More than a decade of work went into this book, even if the actual writing was accomplished in a compressed frenzy during 2012. I thank all of the many colleagues, and especially the clients who have been on a journey of co-discovery with me as we've learned the lessons of digital disruption together. Among those, a few contributors are worthy of special mention here.

A big thank-you to Forrester's founder and CEO, George F. Colony, for building a company that pays people like to me to think and then challenges us to make those thoughts useful to clients. Dennis van Lingen, managing director of Forrester's Marketing & Strategy client group, gave me the green light, in essence letting me disrupt my own role at Forrester by writing this book.

A more direct thanks goes to Senior Vice President of Idea Development Josh Bernoff. His title accurately describes what he helped me accomplish with this manuscript. As coauthor on two of Forrester's previous books, *Groundswell* and *Empowered*, as well as editor of the book *Outside In*, Josh provided invaluable guidance on how to make these ideas work in book form.

I've been fortunate at Forrester to work for managers who believe in the ideas I have been tracking, in some cases for many years. Thanks to Carl Doty, whose passion for disrupting things exceeds even my own. I credit him for listening to me when I claimed that all of these threads tied together into a single concept and then committing time and resources to bring it to life.

I owe a debt of gratitude to former colleague Mark Mulligan, whose passion for healing broken media industries made him the ideal comrade-at-arms. He first pushed me to see that my work constituted a new kind of disruption. I also owe Mark for the title of the first digital disruption report I wrote for Forrester, *The Disruptor's Handbook*.

I work with inspiring and resourceful people. Sarah Rotman Epps is relentless in her pursuit of ideas and as a result is an industry leader in her coverage. Thanks to Sander Rose for coordinating so many interviews and for staying on top of developments in the industry for this and other projects. Annie Corbett provided great support on projects where we learned some of these lessons. And Sara Townsend put me in front of her clients again and again to present, test, and refine the concepts that are in this book. As always, I thank Rachel Birrell, whose sharp editing of most of the reports that led to this book made each of them better, making this book better as well.

I offer a special thank-you to those clients and industry examples who agreed to be interviewed for this book, even the ones that did not make it into the final manuscript. Your willingness to share what you have learned—the good, the bad, and the disruptive—is inspiring. Thank you for your examples and your trust.

Actually getting a book like this done—and in record time, I'm told—requires many willing hands. Thank you to Jens Kueter for rapid turnaround on the graphics and to Liz Menard and Amy Lewis for the website. And it is a pleasure to be working with Erica Sahin once again. If you read this book, thank her.

On the Amazon side, my sincere appreciation to editor David Moldawer for taking a risk on a book that absolutely, positively had to be published in four months instead of eighteen. His input and his diligence were both vital. And thanks to members of his team, Dennelle Catlett and Alicia Criner, who worked on publicity and marketing to make this book reach as many hands and minds as possible.

Thank you to my wife and children, who have always supported my writing. Their many disruptions to my life are the ones I value most. Fingers crossed, team, maybe we can finally take that trip to Disney World!

A final gesture of thanks goes out to the ranks of digital disruptors themselves, those who have internalized technology and have begun constructing a world after their own liking. I sincerely believe that you are on to something and that the rest of us will be better off if we follow.

—James McQuivey,
Cambridge, Massachusetts, October 2012

About the Author

A vice president and principal analyst at Forrester Research, James is the leading analyst tracking the development of digital disruption. He develops consumer models to help companies understand the power of digital consumers and strategy models to help companies in every industry prepare to serve those newly empowered consumers. His meetings with clients have taken him to Oslo, San Diego, Barcelona, Anchorage, and nearly everywhere else on the planet. No matter the locale, he can be found imploring clients to think and act like digital disruptors.

James is in high demand as a speaker, keynoting and contributing to major events like CES as well as private client events. He comments regularly in the *New York Times* and the *Wall Street Journal* and has contributed bylined columns for sites like Harvard Business Review, The Economist, and Forbes. He also appears frequently on news outlets such as CNBC and NPR. James was recently featured in the critically acclaimed documentary *Page One*, which examined the changes in the newsroom at the *New York Times* with the advent of digital news gathering and distribution. He is also a significant contributor to *Stay Tuned*, a new documentary on the future of TV produced by Julia Boorstin at CNBC.

In the fourteen years since he first joined Forrester Research as an online retail analyst, James has opened Forrester's coverage of the automotive and travel industries as well as run the Consumer Technographics research arm of the company—the largest and longest-running survey effort in the world focused on consumer use of and interaction with technology. His analysis of millions of survey responses is what led him to conclude that digital was preparing consumers for something completely different.

James came to Forrester from a happy life in academia. He was a graduate fellow at Syracuse University's S. I. Newhouse School of Public Communications, where he earned his PhD. He also taught at Boston University.

James lives in Needham, Massachusetts, with his wife and the four youngest of their six disruptors.

Notes

Much of the information in this book comes from direct in-person, telephone, and email interviews by the author with the people and representatives of the companies described in the book. Facts and quotes that do not have a note come from these personal interviews.

In these notes, when citing a long web address, we typically use an equivalent address of the form http://forr.com/ddbookX-Y. We created these site references for the convenience of the reader. Enter the web address into your browser and you will be redirected to the appropriate site online.

Please note that as in all cases with web addresses, people sometimes change or remove content that we have cited. Web content cited was visible at the time the book was written.

Many of these citations are Forrester reports. If you are a Forrester client with appropriate access, the cited address will take you to the report page online where you can read or download the full report. If you are not a client or your relationship with Forrester does not include access to the report, you'll see a short excerpt of the report. If you're still interested in the full report, you can sign up to become a client or purchase the report.

CHAPTER 1

1   All of my information about Thomas comes from YouTube and other public sources. Though Thomas was invited to be interviewed for this book, his parents politely declined. Source: http://forr.com/ddbook1-1

2   The Bustin Jieber app has since been updated several times. Source: http://forr.com/ddbook1-2

3   You know you're at least a momentary celebrity when the *Huffington Post* covers you. See "Thomas Suarez, 12-Year-Old Wunderkind, Gives a TED Talk On His Apps" *Huffington Post*, Nov. 15, 2011, http://forr.com/ddbook1-3

4   More than three-fourths of US households have broadband access. Source: Forrester's North American Technographics Benchmark Survey, Q3 2012, N=13,688 US adult householders

5   Patent data compiled from a report by the US Patent and Trademark Office, available at http://forr.com/ddbook1-5

6   See the seminal book *The Innovator's Dilemma,* by Clayton M. Christensen (HarperBusiness, 1997). http://forr.com/ddbook1-6 . Christensen's work on the subject has expanded significantly since the publication of the original. See http://www.claytonchristensen.com/ for more publications and references.

7   We first published this model of the power of digital disruption for Forrester's clients in October of 2011. See the Forrester Report, "The Disruptor's Handbook," by James McQuivey, October 27, 2011, http://forr.com/ddbook1-7

8   According to Apple CEO Tim Cook at the Worldwide Developers Conference 2012. See "Apple: 30B Apps Downloaded, 400M App Store Accounts Set Up" by Don Reisinger, *CNET,* June 11, 2012, http://forr.com/ddbook1-8

9   Taken from the Facebook Securities and Exchange filing, Form S-1, Amendment No. 4, April 23, 2012. See: http://forr.com/ddbook1-9

10 For an overview of Kickstarter's impact on business funding, see "Kickstarter's Funded Projects See Some Stumbles," by Mark Milian, *Bloomberg,* August 21, 2012, http://forr.com/ddbook1-10

CHAPTER 2

1   For the full details of the acquisition, see the press release "Shire to Acquire FerroKin BioSciences, Inc., and Its Phase 2 Iron Chelator Treatment," March 15, 2012, http://forr.com/ddbook2-1

CHAPTER 3

1   For the definitive introduction of the role of free things in the internet economy, see *Free,* by Chris Anderson (Hyperion, 2009), http://forr.com/ddbook3-1

2 For more analysis on the ambition behind the iBooks Author Tool, see "Apple Unveils New iBooks Author Tool, Not Just for Textbooks" by Chris Velazco, *TechCrunch*, January 19, 2012, http://forr.com/ddbook3-2

3 For more on the rise of Kindle millionaires, see "Who Wants To Be a (Kindle) Millionaire?" by Kiri Blakeley, *Forbes*, March 6, 2011, http://forr.com/ddbook3-3

4 Relive those heady days at "Buy.com: How Soon We Forget," by Justin Hibbard, *Businessweek*, January. 25, 2005, http://forr.com/ddbook3-4

5 Listen to Ryan Park, technical operations and infrastructure lead at Pinterest, describe his team's use of AWS in "Pinterest on AWS: Customer Success Story" on YouTube.com, http://forr.com/ddbook3-5

CHAPTER 4

1 Even five more minutes of engagement a day would dramatically alter most companies' customer relationships. See the Forrester Report, "The Disruptor's Handbook," by James McQuivey, October 27, 2011, http://forr.com/ddbook4-1

2 See "Microsoft Kinect Hacked? Already?!" by Jack Loftus, *Gizmodo*, November 7, 2010, http://forr.com/ddbook4-2

3 See how Microsoft began to shift its stand within just weeks of the hack at "Microsoft: I'm a PC, and Kinect Open-source Drivers Were My Idea," by Sean Hollister, *Engadget*, November 20, 2010, http://forr.com/ddbook4-3

CHAPTER 5

1 We first presented the facts about fundamental human needs to Forrester clients in the Forrester Report, "What People Really Need," by James McQuivey, February 4, 2010, http://forr.com/ddbook5-1

2 Facebook hit a billion users about two months before I expected. See "Facebook Surpasses One Billion Users as It Tempts New Markets," by Dave Lee, BBC News, October 5, 2012, http://forr.com/ddbook5-2

3 For the most recent assessment of how much video is added to YouTube each day, see "Frequently Asked Questions," on YouTube.

com, under "How many videos are on YouTube?" http://www.you-tube.com/t/faq

4   Though we all learned it in Psych 101, the original theory was proposed in "A Theory of Human Motivation," by A. H. Maslow, *Psychological Review* no. 50 (1943): 370–398.

5   Many years later—and a year after we published my critique of Maslow—surveys across 123 countries verified that Maslow was wrong about our needs being hierarchical. See "Maslow 2.0: A New and Improved Recipe for Happiness," by Hans Villarica, *The Atlantic*, August 17, 2011, http://forr.com/ddbook5-5

6   The definitive textbook on brain science is by Kandel, Schwartz, and Jessell, now in its fifth edition. In my third-edition copy from graduate school, they wrote, "Each mental process—perceiving, thinking, learning, remembering—seems continuous and indivisible. We experience mental processes as essentially instantaneous, smooth operations. Actually these processes are composed of several independent information-processing components, and even the simplest cognitive task requires the coordination of several distinct brain areas." (p. 15). See the most recent edition, *Principles of Neural Science, 5th edition*, by E. R. Kandel, J. H. Schwartz, and T. M. Jessell (McGraw-Hill, 2012).

7   For a good summary of years of terror management theory research, see "Terror Management Theory of Self-esteem and Cultural Worldviews: Empirical Assessments and Conceptual Refinements," by J. Greenberg, S. Solomon, and T. Pyszczynski, in *Advances in Experimental Social Psychology* no. 29 (1997): 61–136. My own dissertation work built on this theory, tying it to known neural processes and structures. See *Testing the Hardwired for News Theory of Media Surveillance*, by James McQuivey, UMI, 2008.

8   Professor Arthur Aron's research into the neural ties that bind couples together is summarized in "Reinventing Date Night for Long-Married Couples," by Tara Parker-Pope, *New York Times* Well Blog, February 12, 2008, http://forr.com/ddbook5-8

CHAPTER 6

1 We first wrote about innovating the adjacent possible for Forrester's clients in 2011. See the Forrester Report, "Innovating The Adjacent Possible," by James McQuivey, August 4, 2011, http://forr.com/ddbook6-1

2 This is possibly the best book about ideas ever written. See *Where Good Ideas Come From: The Natural History of Innovation*, by Steven Johnson (Riverhead Hardcover, 2010). http://forr.com/ddbook6-2

3 These iPad precursors and more like them are presented and cited in more detail in the Forrester Report, "Innovating The Adjacent Possible," by James McQuivey, August 4, 2011, http://forr.com/ddbook6-3

4 For a more complete discussion of the power that accrues to customers when switching costs fall so precipitously, see the Forrester Report, "Competitive Strategy In The Age Of The Customer," by Josh Bernoff, June 6, 2011, http://forr.com/ddbook6-4

CHAPTER 7

1 See more about the importance of customer experience in a digitally disruptive age in *Outside In: The Power of Putting Customers at the Center of Your Business*, by Harley Manning and Kerry Bodine (New Harvest, 2012). Book site at http://outsidein.forrester.com/

2 There are many demo videos to choose from, but one of the most complete is "Calabasas City Spotlight: FaceCake Marketing Technologies, Inc." on YouTube, http://forr.com/ddbook7-2

3 We first wrote about the emerging importance of the minutes of engagement metric for Forrester clients in the Forrester Report, "The Disruptor's Handbook," by James McQuivey, October 27, 2011, http://forr.com/ddbook7-3

4 The CBSP method is a product-focused tool derived from the POST method for planning social media use first proposed in *Groundswell: Winning in a World Transformed by Social Technologies*, by Charlene Li and Josh Bernoff (Harvard Business Review Press, 2008). Book site at http://forrester.com/groundswell

CHAPTER 8

1 For a transcript of the interview in which John Spinale described Disney's gaming challenges, see "John Spinale Navigates Disney's Push into Social Gaming." Interview by Evan Killham, *Venture Beat*, July 20, 2012, http://forr.com/ddbook8-1

2 To see how far Disney has come from its first disruptive steps: "Imangi Taps Disney/Pixar to Launch 'Temple Run: Brave' Ahead of Movie Launch," by Jordan Crook, *TechCrunch*, June 5, 2012, http://forr.com/ddbook8-2

CHAPTER 9

1 Read public statements about Amazon's approach to development, including its reliance on two-pizza teams, at "Amazon's CTO: 'Amazon Is a Technology Company. We Just Happen to Do Retail'," by Brad McCarty, *The Next Web Insider*, October 5, 2011, http://forr.com/ddbook9-01

2 See this rapid development experiment yourself in "Nordstrom Innovation Lab: Sunglass iPad App Case Study" on YouTube.com, September 28, 2011, http://forr.com/ddbook9-02

CHAPTER 10

1 See *Free Agent Nation*, by Daniel Pink (Business Plus, 2002), http://forr.com/ddbook10-1

2 Oh, and it's highly likely this next Oprah wouldn't even be a person, but would instead be a piece of adaptive, intelligent software, but that's a topic for another book.

Index